Sporting [illegible]

Stoke-on-Trent: European City of Sport 2016

Edited by Peter Hooper

First published 2017

Cox Bank Publishing Limited

Brook House, Brook Lane,
Coxbank, Crewe, CW3 0EU

The Dudson Centre
Hope Street, Hanley
Stoke-on-Trent ST1 5DD

email: info@coxbankpublishing.com
web: www.coxbankpublishing.com

ISBN 978-0-9956672-1-1

Printed and bound in the UK

"The way to succeed is to try"

Meg Higgins, from *My Dancing Poem*

"So I started and I was enjoying it so I kept going and going so I've become this good"

Harry Smith, from *Wheelchair Basketball*

This book is dedicated to the sporting heroes of Stoke-on-Trent: past, current and future

Contents

	Acknowledgements		7
	Preface	Terry Follows	10
	Forward	Peter Hooper	13
1.	2016: A Sporting Year	Peter Hooper	16
2.	It All Started With...	Andy Baggaley	25
3.	My Story - So Far...	Zara Bailey	29
4.	My Dream	Jessica Barnhouse	36
5.	The Race of Truth: Racing the Mersey Roads 24 Hour TT	Andy Barratt	38
6.	Charlie and the Karvan go to Middleport Park...	Peter Hooper	41
	Dance	*Meg Higgins*	*45*
	Running	*Sara Morris*	*45*
	Roller-skating	*Penny Morris*	*46*
	Roller-skating	*Eadie Morris*	*46*
	Football	*Marvin Molloy*	*47*
	Basketball	*Maddison Taia Molloy*	*47*
	Gymnastics	*Mackayla Rhodes*	*48*
	Ice-skating	*Gemma Woodworth*	*48*
	Mountain Biking	*Amy Merry*	*49*
	Ice-skating	*Karen Firkins*	*49*
	Roller-skating	*Tia Firkins*	*50*
	Trampolining	*Chloe Tams*	*50*
	Football	*Emmett*	*51*
7.	My Cat & Fiddle Challenge	Erin Boddice	52
8.	Paralympic journey	Jenny Booth	55
9.	The Sloth: The Roaches HVS 5a/b	Duncan Bourne	60
10.	Potteries Adventures (co-author Georgia Oldham)	Tom Brennan	63
11.	Peter William Bunn, 72	Anthony Bunn	68
12.	The Golden Archers	Daniel Cartwright	76
13.	My Journey	Lucas Christer	80
14.	Up For the Challenge: From the Start	Jeremy Cliffe	82
15.	A Sporting Life	Viv Cotton	84

16.	Ready: Racket Up	Joey Courchene	88
17.	Happy High Ropes	Kirsten Else	90
18.	Memories of My Father, Sir Stan	Jean Gough	92
19.	Aggression vs Fierce Fun: The Fine Line	Mowenna Hastings	99
20.	A White Water Ride - or a Life in Sport	Andrew Heaward	102
21.	My Dancing Poem (again!)	Meg Higgins	109
22.	The Stoke-on-Trent City of Sport UK Triathlon	Peter Hooper	110
23.	The Love of My Life	Ron Hughes	118
24.	My Sporting Story – Athletics	Emma Jackson	121
25.	Carrying a Torch	Glenn James	125
26.	A Few Memories of Klondike Bill	Barbara Jones	132
27.	Trip of a Lifetime	Mary Joynson	135
28.	Tutus, Tears and the Awful Tiger Costume	Becky Latham	138
29.	Fresh Air for Body and Soul	Maurice Leyland	141
30.	The 'Arf of Two 'Arfs	Nicola Lingley-Heath	143
31.	Charlie and the Karvan go to Northwood…	Peter Hooper	152
	Jujitsu	*Kyle Onza*	*153*
	Football	*Jay Sandhu*	*153*
	Football	*Josh Hampton*	*155*
	Hill-walking	*Daniel Hannan*	*155*
	Canoeing	*Tayibah*	*156*
	Canoeing	*Safa*	*156*
32.	Sailing	Sophie Longmore	158
33.	The Stoke-on-Trent Triathlon	Gianni Loska	160
34.	My Sporting Story	Janet Mason	162
35.	"You Should Be Dead"	Nigel Moore	164
36.	The Lord Mayor's Sporting Story	Anthony Munday	167
37.	City of Sport 2016	Frank Murphy	170
38.	I Love My Sport	Gilbert Owen	173
39.	What Sport Means to Me	Jonathan Pace	176
40.	parkrun: Celebrating in the Rain	Ruth Parsons	179
41.	Like Paddling Through Your Own Wildlife Documentary	Zoe Robinson	181

42. One Day That Changed My Life	Ken Rushton	186
43. Portrait of an Artist as a Working Man (Dave Proudlove)	Steve Shaw	189
44. The Match	Ilenia Sims	192
45. Recollections of Stoke Speedway	Pat Sinclair	194
46. My Sporting Story – Squash	Angela Smith	198
47. The Chirp	Jeremy Snape	200
48. It Seemed a Good Idea at the Time	Dave Steele	202
49. My Sporting Story - Time for a Change	Liz Tideswell	206
50. A Day in the Life of a Ball	David Tierney	209
51. Road to Africa	Matthew Wilcock	211
52. Charlie and the Karvan go to Hanley…	Peter Hooper	227
Dance	*Matthew Byatt*	*229*
Dance	*Donna Stanway*	*230*
Swimming	*Lillian Beardmore*	*231*
Rugby Tots	*Helen Stennings*	*231*
Paragliding	*Nathan Hill*	*232*
Athletics	*Ben Adamson*	*232*
Gymnastics	*Mia Beardmore*	*233*
Wheelchair Basketball	*Harry Smith*	*234*
Running	*Angela Marie Tyler*	*236*
Bouldering	*Cathi Ferrer*	*237*
Athletics	*Matt Fry*	*237*
Running	*Craig Smith*	*238*
Wheelies	*Melissa Walker*	*239*
Horse-riding	*Carla*	*239*
Wheelchair Basketball	*George Chapman*	*240*
Goalball	*Peter Doyle*	*242*
53. Summerbank Primary School	Peter Hooper	243
Jannath - My First Gymnastics Lessons (Hannah Stanway)		*244*
Amy - My First Gymnastics Lessons (Alessandra Lombardi)		*246*
54. Afterword – A View From ACES Europe	John Swanson	248
Photograph and Illustration Credits		250

Acknowledgements

As this book goes to press there have been some 500 contributions to the Stoke-on-Trent *Sporting Stories* project and to related initiatives: from individuals, sports clubs, community groups, care homes and from schools. Space doesn't allow me to thank all the individual authors by name here, but I can say that it has been quite a challenge to sift through all the pieces and select those which have made it into print! We continue to add entries to the *Sporting Stories* website www.sportingstories.com and to parallel collections covering the Potters 'Arf, the Cat & Fiddle Challenge and projects with local schools.

I would particularly like to thank the 80 or so authors represented in this book, covering a wonderful cross-section of Stoke-on-Trent sports, communities and generations. Each piece is either 'as submitted' or only very lightly edited, so that each contributor's voice and style shines through. It makes for an eclectic mix but I hope is the better for it. For some contributions, particularly from the three workshops we ran, we have transcribed a conversation, but as far as possible we have adhered to the principle that contributors submit their own writing about their own sporting lives.

The *Sporting Stories* project has by its very nature been highly collaborative and I and Cox Bank Publishing have received enormous support through the year in making it happen. First and foremost has been the support from the Stoke-on-Trent European City of Sport team, and the City Council. Angela Smith, Chair of the City of Sport Local Organising Committee (LOC), has been a supporter from Day One. A grant awarded by the LOC has part-funded this project and made it possible. From the City Council, Terry Follows, Cabinet Member for Greener City, Development and Leisure; former Lord Mayor Jean Bowers; and current Lord Mayor Anthony Munday have all been enormously helpful in their support. Michelle Vorel-Adams, Strategic Manager for Leisure, Culture and Museums and her team have provided a wealth of practical help throughout the year. In particular, Andrew Heaward, General Manager Leisure has very actively supported *Sporting Stories* and his help and thoughtful counsel have been invaluable. Andrew and the City of Sport team of Kate Beer, Lotta Bowers, Geoff Beadle, Jo Haywood, Ash Holland and Neal Morrell have helped make *Sporting Stories* an integral part of the City of Sport initiative and have facilitated many links and opportunities for the project. I would also like to thank all the members of the LOC for their support. The organisations on the LOC are listed on page 14.

Thanks are also due the following for their support and encouragement: Chris Austin, Dave Bartram, Norman Bassett, Amelia Bilson, Jenny Booth, Tom Brennan, Cameron Brown, Anthony Bunn, John Capper, Jason Christer, Jake Cliffe, Andy Cooke, Gareth Cowlin, Andy Flower, Danny Flynn, Jon French, Jan Garner, Neil Gilson, Jane Gratton, Mick Hall, Vanessa Hamilton, Angela James, Glenn James, Peter Jones, Wendy Jones, Warren Kelsall, John Mainwaring, Ian Marsden, Janet Mason, Deb McAndrew, Frank Murphy, Jonathan Pace, Harry Pointon, Dave Proudlove, Ben Rigby, Jim Rowley, Ken Rushton, Sue Rushton, Louise Rutherford, Don Shelley, Yvonne Skipper, Andrew Stanier, Glen Stoker, Lee Taylor, Liz Tideswell, Pete Twilley, Emma Dawson Varughese, Keith Wales, John Webbe, Dave Wellings, Paul Williams, Sara Williams, and the VAST team at the Dudson Centre in Hanley.

Some particular groups deserve special mention: for their help in schools' engagement or running pilot projects I'd like to thank Helen Moors of oPEn, Nigel Edwards of Stoke School Sport Partnership and the Excel Academy, Abi Falconer of Summerbank Primary School, Kate Schonau and Lisa Wainwright of Hillside Primary School, and Tom Hughes of St Joseph's College. St Joe's had a whole school *Sporting Stories* competition, which resulted in a mountain of 250 submissions arriving at Cox Bank Publishing's office! See chapters 4, 12, 17, 32, 33, 44, 50 and 53 for contributions from St Joe's, Hillside and Summerbank.

As the project grew through the year, I started recruiting volunteer sports correspondents to help me track down good stories in particular sports. The first of these is Steve Dyster who has done sterling work in finding inspirational cycling stories, several of which are included in the book. Thank you Steve.

Local writing groups and individual writers have been a source of help and inspiration. Thanks to June Palmer and colleagues at City Voices; Peter and Jan Coleborn and others at Renegade Writers; Phil Williams et al at the Stoke Poetry Stanza; and to Tom Palmer, Giovanni 'Spoz' Esposito and Emma Purshouse for their support and encouragement. And also to Emma George and Janet Thursfield at Hanley City Central Library for introducing me to many of these folk.

Stoke-on-Trent is blessed with an abundance of creative talent and it has been a particular pleasure to work with local artists, who have been generous in their support of *Sporting Stories*. I'm delighted to be able to showcase a number of them in this book: Gaz Williams in particular but also Kate Ackley, Duncan Bourne, Simon Chubb, Paine Proffitt, Steve Shaw, Charlie Walker – and the incredibly talented young artist Lucas Christer. Thanks also to local galleries Airspace, The Art Dept and Barewall for providing help and/or inspiration, and to Appetite, the Hot Air Literary Festival and the LiveAge Festival for their engagement.

Student volunteers and work experience students have provided invaluable support over the course of the year, and I would like to acknowledge the contribution of Natalia Falacinska (Newcastle-under-Lyme College), Katie Pickering and Becky Latham (Stoke-on-Trent Sixth Form College), and Taranpreet Sangha (Keele University). Thanks also to Staffordshire University Cartoon and Comic Art degree students Natalie Burgher, Alessandra Lombardi, Sam Megaw, Phoenix Morris and Hannah Stanway for their contributions. One other group of students deserves special mention and that is the Stoke City Community Trust's National Citizen Service volunteer group from July 2016 – thanks to them all for a sterling week's service.

And finally, thanks to my wife (and co-director) Vanessa and to Ben and Beki for all their support and encouragement, and for believing in me and the project.

Peter Hooper, Cox Bank Publishing

Preface

Terry Follows

Councillor and Cabinet member for Greener City, Development and Leisure
Stoke-on-Trent City Council

It gives me great pleasure to write the preface to this collection of stories about sport in and around Stoke-on-Trent, the UK's European City of Sport for 2016. As a city, we were enormously proud to be awarded our City of Sport status by ACES Europe (the European Capitals and Cities of Sport Federation).

ACES award European City of Sport status to cities with a population between 25,000 and 500,000, which demonstrate a passion to sport at every level. And if there is one thing Stoke-on-Trent has, it is certainly passion about sport – at every level from our two professional football clubs; Olympic and Paralympic stars; current, former and future world champions; through to people simply enjoying sport and outdoor pastimes as a way of keeping fit.

To be awarded City of Sport status, Stoke-on-Trent had to show how our sporting activity supported the values of ACES Europe, which are

- Enjoyment in exercise
- Willingness to achieve
- Community cohesion
- Improvement of health
- Fair play

The city's recognition by ACES Europe was down to our belief in sport as a power for good; and the drive of partners to regenerate Stoke-on-Trent, boost civic pride and raise the city's profile through sport. All of this, combined with our focus on health and wellbeing, was the key to success - along with a desire to involve the whole community.

Everyone has had the chance to be involved in our year as European City of Sport. Whether it has been through attending an event, organising a community festival, or volunteering at a sports session people of all ages have jumped at the chance to help make 2016 a truly spectacular year!

Through the year, we have supported a range of programmes and initiatives and this book is a result of one such project, developed in partnership with local social enterprise Cox Bank Publishing. Sporting Stories is described in more detail in the Forward to this book, but suffice to say it has succeeded in getting people of all ages and across all parts of the city to put down in their own words what they love about sport.

However, it's not just about 2016. Our European City of Sport year is just the start, and Stoke-on-Trent will continue to build on this year's success. 2017 and 2018 (and beyond) will see lots of ongoing initiatives to embed the good work of this year and to build a City of Sport legacy to be proud of. And on that front, I'm delighted to say that this book is only the first of a Sporting Stories series, with further volumes celebrating more writers and more sports appearing in 2017 and 2018.

I hope you enjoy the 2016 book.

Hang on! Leave the writing till afterwards!
Scanlon

Forward

Peter Hooper

A little bit of history. Back in July 2015 Stoke-on-Trent was awarded European City of Sport (ECoS) status for 2016 and by a happy coincidence just a month or so earlier Cox Bank Publishing Limited had been established as a social enterprise specialising in publishing writing about sport and physical activity. Two separate events but linked by a shared ambition to celebrate and encourage sport as a power for good. And perfect timing for the 'sporting stories' initiative I was planning to launch locally as Cox Bank Publishing's first project.

Cox Bank Publishing's initial approach to the ECoS team at Stoke-on-Trent City Council was simply to ask if we could use the ECoS logo with our project, but after a couple of meetings they were as excited as I was at the prospect of a more ambitious plan to develop a website and a subsequent book capturing local writing about sport.

In the eighteen months that elapsed between those initial meetings and the publication of this book, the original simple request to use the logo has turned into a much deeper collaboration and partnership. I am very grateful to the ECoS team, and to the Local Organising Committee, for all their support with the project, which has become an integral part of the City of Sport portfolio. That wider portfolio was made possible by the support it received from the Leader, Deputy Leader and Cabinet of the Council. I also gratefully acknowledge a grant Cox Bank Publishing was awarded by the LOC to help develop the project, with the objective of delivering three *Sporting Stories* books over three years: 2016, 2017 and 2018. The list of organisations which make up the LOC is illuminating, showing the strength of support for the project across the City and beyond, to which you can add engagement from across the City via clubs, community groups, businesses and charities.

The Stoke-on-Trent 2016 European City of Sport Local Organising Committee comprises:

- Sport England
- Stoke City FC
- Port Vale FC
- Staffordshire Chambers of Commerce
- YMCA North Staffordshire
- SASSOT (Sport Across Staffordshire & Stoke – representing local sports clubs)
- Stoke-on-Trent City Council
- Newcastle-under-Lyme Borough Council
- Staffordshire Moorlands Borough Council
- Staffordshire University
- Keele University
- Stoke College
- Andrew Stanier (representing Stoke-on-Trent schools)
- VAST (covering Voluntary and Community Groups, Charities & Social Enterprises)

Sporting Stories – Stoke-on-Trent is the first of the series of books celebrating sport in and around the City. The idea is a simple one: to get people who are engaged in sport and physical activity to write in their own words and in their own voice what it is they get from being active. We were hoping to get a variety of stories (short accounts of races, events, matches, memories, wins, losses, mishaps and more) covering a variety of sports - and I hope you'll agree that we've certainly met that objective.

Sporting Stories originally started out being aimed at club-level amateur sports people – keen sports club members were very much the initial target audience – but conversations with the ECoS team have led to the scope being broadened significantly to include schools, community groups, care home residents and a generally much wider spread of contributors, so much so that that our youngest author is four and our oldest is well over eighty!

Pulling together this first book of *Sporting Stories* has been a bit of a roller-coaster ride. There was nothing at the start of the project to say that enough people would want to write about their love of sport, or would be able to write entertainingly enough to create stories that might inspire others to take up sport or try a new activity – a key aim of the project. What we particularly wanted were personal experiences - stories of sporting glory or personal achievement, wins and losses, the motivation and inspiration behind epic challenges. And we've got that in spades – with contributors ranging from world champions and world record holders through to people who just love to get out and enjoy the outdoors. Most of the stories are quite short, which we hope will make the book something to easily dip into and enjoy on a regular basis. Over twenty sports are covered in this first volume and there are plenty more to come for the 2017 edition.

An added pleasure of compiling and editing this book has been the discovery (for me) that Stoke-on-Trent not only has a thriving and engaging community of writers, but that it also has a wealth of artists capturing sport and sporting history in their work. I am hugely grateful to a number of key individuals (listed in the Acknowledgements) for allowing me to reproduce some of their work as illustrations for stories.

Happy reading.

1. 2016: A Sporting Year

Peter Hooper

It's a minute past midnight and the New Year has just begun. 1st January 2016. Auld lang syne is blasting out of the TV and our front room is full of family hugging (or in a couple of cases just holding each other up), wishing each other well for the coming year and making resolutions for the coming year.

I normally make lots of New Year resolutions and then rigidly adhere to them for somewhere between a week and a month. But this year is different. I've got a variation on the usual "I must do more sport and be more active" resolution - which is to try and do a different sport or event every week, for a year. I round the number down to 50, to give me a little bit of wiggle room.

Why the challenge? Because this is 'City of Sport' year. Or more precisely, 'Stoke-on-Trent European City of Sport 2016' year. And I'm responsible for an element of the delivery of 'The Year' for the year – the Sporting Stories project. Which means during 2016 what I have to do is get a few people I already know, and a lot of people I don't know, to write stuff for me – entertaining or moving stuff about their life and the place of sport in it. Oh, and not just to get lots of people to write, but across as many different sports as possible... How hard can that be?

Hence the resolution – to try and meet new groups and clubs to ask people to write. I and the City of Sport team will be using other channels as well to encourage contributors, but getting out there and trying new activities or new events strikes me as a good route to get stories - and one which might get me fitter.

Here's how the year went:

January

Not quite a local sporting story but on 2nd January I kick off the year by going with my daughter to watch **rugby union**: Sale Sharks beat Wasps 15-9 in Salford on a bitterly cold Saturday evening. The rest of the month sees me try out my first **parkrun** – a 5k in Hanley - plus I do some **wild swimming** at Hatchmere, a Cheshire mere. Even in a wetsuit it's freezing, but there are hardier swimmers than me just in skins (that means just in a swimming costume, not just a birthday suit). On 21st I go to watch Glynn Terry train at Northwood Stadium: a former Paralympic swimmer and now looking for GB qualification in **shot put**. On the 30th – the day of the big launch event for the European City of Sport - I marshal at parkrun, watch Longton RUFC come unstuck against Bromsgrove and drop into the Hulton Abbey Amateur **Boxing** Club's 30th anniversary celebrations. At the launch event I meet friends old and new and see some stunning **dance** routines, plus hundreds of sports stars in the making parade round the Northwood athletics track. No shortage of potential authors there.

February

On the 5th I go to the Sir Stanley Matthews Coaching Foundation's **gala dinner**, mingling with the great and the good of local sport; the 6th sees me up in the Lake District to watch **ChillSwim** relays in Lake Windermere; and the 7th I compete in the Alsager 5 **road race**. On the 11th it's the launch event for the wonderful '**Run for Fun**' initiative, which will take place in May; and on 15th I meet local playwright Deb McAndrew to talk sport and writing.

The 23rd is the launch of the City of Sport '**Talented Athletes Scheme**' – and I meet some amazing stars of the future. And other stars – I think this is the first time I meet local Paralympian swimming gold medallist and world record holder Jenny Booth, a future contributor and big supporter of the project. On 29th it's the **launch event** of Sporting Stories itself and a chance to thank supporters and early contributors – contributors like Angela Smith, former world squash champion; and Emma Jackson, England international 800m runner and former world's fastest junior. I am truly humbled by the support the project is getting. The Sentinel runs a piece on the launch – all good publicity.

March

4th: I meet Tink Hastings, a coach at Stoke Spitfires **Wheelchair Basketball** club. It sounds a great sport, must try it one day. A **fell race** on 6th – 'Cloud 9' at Congleton. Brilliant to be doing some fell-running again. There's a fantastic descent where I'm right at the limit and only narrowly avoid splatting myself against a tree. On 11th I meet Ian Marsden, **paracanoeist** and all round super-star. There's a whole book (and a film) to be made of Ian's life – an outstanding sportsman at multiple disciplines and general good bloke. 16th: I go to a talk by Mandy Mitten, a local business woman just back from competing in the Round the World **Clipper Race**. Terrifying images of huge seas and crazily listing yachts. 19th sees me spectating at Hanley Town FC, a great local **football** club, completely rooted in its community and putting a huge amount back into the game. 21st and it's a '**Change 4 Life**' school sports festival – wonderful to see pupils from the Excel Academy mentoring and coaching primary school children. Excel pupils True Machin and Jodie Collins become Sporting Stories roving reporters for the day. And another **parkrun** to close the month.

April

Things start hotting up. 3rd is the KMF Newcastle **10k**, which I run. I realise I'm starting to get to know a decent number of local runners across a range of clubs: StokeFIT, Newcastle AC, Potters Trotters, Trentham RC and more. Great people. 6th and a City of Sport film showing by the **Staffordshire Film Archive**, run by Ray Johnson MBE. I realise what a tremendous sporting history Stoke-on-Trent has, across so many sports: football, obviously, but boxing, cricket, athletics, cycling... If Sporting Stories does even a tiny bit to help capture sporting legacy in the city, it will be an enormous privilege to have been involved. 10th and I finally get to have a go at **wheelchair basketball** with Stoke Spitfires. Coach Andy Flowers explains a few rules and I'm off. Brilliant fun, despite being mercilessly 'taken out' by young tyros in their wheelchairs. Respect. 22nd and I take guests Liz and Jon Tideswell to the 66Winners **Gala Dinner** in the King's Hall, Stoke. Amazing to be stood with Gordon Banks - what a gentleman - and his fellow world cup winners.

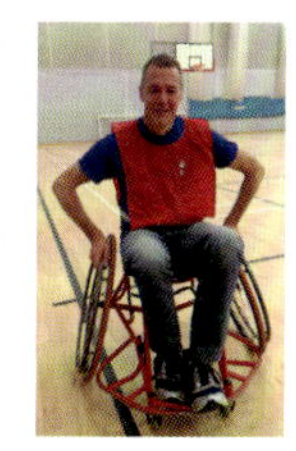

May

I'm certainly getting to meet lots of sportspeople and find out about new sports, but my New Year's Resolution is definitely looking challenging. Still, I rack up another new sport on 4th when I join Trentham **Outriggers** Club for a jaunt on the lake. Lovely place, lovely crew. I lose a couple of weeks when we have a family holiday to visit our daughter, who is studying in Montpellier. Though as luck would have it, the weekend that we arrive, Montpellier is hosting the FISE World Series Extreme Sports Festival, so I rack up **BMX**, **skate-boarding**, **kayaking**, **wake-boarding**, **in-line skating**, **mountain biking** and... **scooters**. No, I didn't know it was an extreme sport either, but it's great to watch the death- and gravity-defying kids on all the various ramps. FISE Stoke-on-Trent anyone? Back in England in time to sound out the Hanley Economic on a Potters 'Arf book idea on 19th and then that evening attend the **Stoke-on-Trent Sports Personality of the Year Awards**. Outstanding. The area is blessed with so much sporting talent and nearly all of it is in the King's Hall in Stoke. Frank Murphy, another contributor, wins Coach of the Year. Adam Burgess, world U23 canoe slalom champion wins Sports Personality of the Year

and I have a good chat with him about his sporting journey. On the 21st the City of Sport '**Run for Fun**' takes place all across the city. I run at Hanley parkrun; Staffs University (where I win); the Willows Primary School (soundly beaten by lots of littlies); and Northwood Stadium. The 28th is the first of three **Corporate Cups** of sport in the city: Football.

June

Off to a cracking start, having a coffee on 1st at Trentham Lake with John Court, 1972 Olympic canoeist and 2014 World **Outrigger** Championship silver medallist. On 2nd it's the Pearl Izumi City Series **cycling** race in Hanley and on 5th it's back to Trentham Lake to watch

the **rowing** club regatta. Trentham again, but the Gardens this time, on 7th to have coffee with the running legend and former GB **Marathon** coach Don Shelley. 10th and I'm at the Stoke-on-Trent Hot Air Literary Festival to hear Graham Fowler talk about his England **cricket** career. The 12th comes round quickly and with very little training in the tank I do the Potters 'Arf **half marathon**. Stunning event and crowds reminiscent of the London Marathon, three or four deep in places. More cycling on 18th as the **Women's Tour** hits Hanley – great to see Lizzie Armistead in action. Finally for June, on 27th I get to see more emerging sporting talent at the North Stoke Schools Sports Partnership **Awards evening**.

July

3rd arrives and with it the Potteries **Marathon**. My legs are still tired from the 'Arf, so I'm pleased to get round in under four-and-a-half hours, but my feet are shot. I get a bit of open water **swimming** done during the month at a new (for me) venue: Hanmer Mere in Shropshire. I do the odd run but what with a number of writing workshops, community events and some family commitments the only other significant event I manage in the month is the 30th and the River Dee **1k swim**. Must do better...

August

Now that the school holidays have arrived the European City of Sport swings into gear with dramatic effect. **StreetGames**, **City Adventures**, **ParkLives**, **PING** and the **Potteries Tennis League** have things on constantly, and an innovative **Canoe Heritage Trail** is well under way. I check out the City Adventures **climbing** wall at Tunstall Park on 4th and rediscover that I truly am a wimp when it comes to even quite moderate heights. Good to see the PING **table tennis** in full swing alongside the wall. On the 6th I marshal at the Hanley **parkrun** and watch the Lord Mayor send a good luck message to TeamGB for the Rio Olympics; then a spot of **Nordic Walking** at Keele with local social enterprise Human-Nature Escapes; and finally catch some **volleyball** with Newcastle Staffs Volleyball Club at Betley Show. I should have rested my legs: the 7th brings the Leek **Half Marathon**, organised by local running stalwarts Ken Rushton and Mick Hall. It's hot and hilly and the Potteries Marathon is still in my legs. Tough day... On 8th I pop across from the office to Forest Park to see the City Adventures canoes and **kayaks** in action and on 9th it's the kayaks and climbing wall at Middleport Park. An evening lake **swim** at Hanmer on 12th and then a big day on 13th with a City of Sport Community Festival back at Middleport Park, with lots on including **lacrosse**. This is followed by a StreetGames Festival at Northwood Stadium on 17th – football, **American football**, climbing and more. On the 24th I meet heroes (and **goalkeepers**) new and old when Jack Butland and Gordon Banks unveil a statue of Gordon at Newcastle-under-Lyme College.

27th brings my busiest day yet on IAmTeamGB day, where I try and attend as many sporting events as possible across Stoke-on-Trent. Hanley **parkrun** is first up, then **Nordic Walking** at Trentham Lake, then the **gym** and pool **swimming** at Nuffield Health in Stoke. Northwood Stadium is next, for table tennis, a 400m **sprint** round the track (not sure 1:29.96 counts as a sprint), watch some **long jump** training sessions and finish with Stoke-Staffs **Boxing** Club back in Hanley. Having run out of Stoke events I try and catch some karate in Market Drayton but end up watching a local derby **cricket** match instead. Great day! And the month isn't over yet – Biddulph on 27th to chat to Sporting Communities at their SPACE **play** day and finally another spot of open water **swimming** at Hanmer on 31st, where by chance I meet Lizzie Tench, world #1 paratriathlete. She swims the length of the lake in the time it takes me to doggy paddle about 50 yards. She also talks me into entering September's Stoke-on-Trent UK Triathlon event...

September

Unbelievably, my first big **cycle ride** of the year: the Potteries Sportive on 4th. It's a fantastic route but I suffer horribly on zero training. On the 6th I try out some **canoeing** with the Potteries Paddlers on Rudyard Lake and eventually master the S-stroke Ray Mears style. 10th brings another big sporting festival, this time the Paralympics UK Festival in Hanley. Jenny Booth, gold-medal winning Paralympian, is guest of honour and an absolute star. I get to try **hand-cycling**, **goalball, boccia**, **rowing** and **archery** and meet dozens of inspiring individuals making light of their disabilities. 17th sees me back out on Trentham Lake at the Corporate Cup of **Dragon Boat** Racing. A brilliant day playing at being pirates, with some serious

racing thrown in too. And then back at the Lake, but in it this time, on 25th, for the Stoke-on-Trent **Triathlon**. My first ever triathlon, and my toughest day of the year yet. The Lake feels cold at 16 degrees and I struggle to finish the swim (let alone the bike and then the run). Finally, the 28th sees me in Birmingham doing research at the Pat Benson **Boxing** Academy.

October

More **boxing** research on 6th with Impact Boxing and Scott Lawton, two-time English lightweight champion. 16th and it's another **cycle challenge**

– this time the Cat & Fiddle event, starting and finishing at Rourke's bike shop in Cobridge. One of my favourite events and a regular annual outing for me. Wet, then foggy, then windy, then sunny, it's a grand day out. Other than that, it's a quiet month on the sporting front: just open water **swimming** every few days to keep acclimatised and the odd **run**.

November

1st of the month and a **swim** – pretty much the only sport I do all month, with a dip at Hanmer a couple of times a week to train for December's International Winter Swimming Association's gala event in Lake Windermere. The temperature drops. And drops. It's sub-5 degrees by 29th.

December

Another first day of the month **swim** (the next one on 1st will be a New Year's Day dip to see in 2017). The water temperature briefly drops below 3 degrees. 10th December and **ChillSwim** finally arrives. Windermere is a balmy 7.3 degrees and actually feels (relatively) warm. The relay team I'm in comes third in its heat, but we have a riot. There are seven Chester

Frosties teams in the pool: the reindeers, snowy owls, dolphins, polar bears, turkeys, penguins and Arctic seals. Worthy of a Planet Earth documentary.

And that's my year done. I'll call the tally of events and sports approximately 50 and say that's job done. Until next year: there's a 2017 Sporting Stories volume to be compiled!

2. It All Started With...

Andy Baggaley

It all started with being diagnosed with Multiple Sclerosis, a debilitating illness that can take over your life, I was lucky, told that I have what's called relapsing remitting MS. The best kind I suppose if you have to have it.

MS affects your stamina and I was told that I would not have the stamina I used to, and they were right. For years especially in summer time I would be like I'd just been unplugged, no energy whatsoever and it wasn't getting any better. I was rather fed up with it, so I decided to try to do something. So I bought a bike, a mountain bike.

Work was a ten mile trip one way, and so I thought I would start there. It took me nearly an hour to get to work and I was absolutely shattered and pouring with sweat, but I did it. After a ten hour shift (nights) I had to pedal back, I felt an overwhelming sense of achievement as well as knackered. Some said I was mad but I hope I inspired many others, as later that year three or four blokes from work bought bikes through the cycle to work scheme, and started doing the same.

Not everyone kept it up, going back to their cars after the first attempt. Giving up more like because they were unfit and it was hard work at first, but perseverance pays off keeping at it made each time easier. I didn't do every day to start, with maybe two or three times a week. But every time seemed to get easier.

This is now a regular commute for me and friend Tony, who I meet up with on the way and we cycle together to work. I was beginning to enjoy it wanting more and more, so much I found the local leisure rides run by Sustrans volunteer Mike Barr. I took my daughter on them too, and they were great. Not only are they very social, but they show you all the cycle network around the city, that is safe keeping you off main roads. It was very interesting to know where you can get from or to not ever touching a main road it really opened my eyes, and Mike is an encyclopaedia of local knowledge.

I got to know Mike quite well and was hungry for more miles. He told me of a group he was in called North Staffs Cycling, and told me they went on longer rides on a Wednesday and Sunday. Well Wednesday was my regular day off so we arranged to meet for a ride, and I bought my friend Tony from work with me.

Now these guys were not young, most retired some in their late sixties. They were all on road or race bikes, and we were on heavy mountain bikes. We went on a seventy-four mile ride with these guys and it was great, except for the route back which went through Hanchurch woods. This is quite hilly with some good climbs, and we did struggle. We were both knackered and we just wanted it to stop, and the two guys who were going our way just left us young studs in the dust and waited for us at the end of the road. Being out-ridden by guys twenty years older than us, I was flabbergasted by their stamina and strength to carry on as they did. They did say we did well to do that kind of mileage on our mountain bikes, and we did enjoy it. So much so that I talked my Mrs around to letting me get a road bike, and I would regularly join them on a Wednesday for a ride. Oh yes! It is a lot easier on a road bike than a mountain bike.

I now go out with friends from work, and my family for rides. Three of us from work went out last month, John, Tony and myself. It was suggested by John that we ride all along the canal towpaths to Liverpool, and that's exactly what we did. But on the way up I was in front riding along a nonexistent towpath, (it was just a narrow strip of grass), and all I heard from behind was "arrrrrooooo" SPLASH! I spun my head around just in time to see John coming out of the water with his bike above his head, just like he was holding Excalibur. Yep John had gone forward somersault into the canal. He didn't see the concrete block in the grass and well, it was funny, especially when a woman who had heard his screams from across the road comes across and offered him a towel and some dry shorts. He kindly refused as they were... PINK!

We did get to Liverpool, well Runcorn just outside Liverpool and we caught the train back. Bloody expensive you really need to book in advance to get the cheaper rates.

I try to get out as much as I can, with my mates John and Tony from work. We did Ashbourne, Buxton and Leek one glorious sunny day this year, remember the one! We like to do charity rides through the year, including the Dougie Mac Llangollen ride which is about 110 miles. I did this ride the first time last year with John and Tony, I rode it for my father who had died a couple of months previous from cancer and Alzheimer's. It was the furthest any of us had ridden. We collected nearly seven hundred pounds between us that year.

This year Mike joined us and another friend from work, Richard who had only ever done sixty miles once. He did really well, and yep he made it all the way.

Next year I will only be doing the fifty-mile ride, as my fifteen year old daughter wants to have a go so I said I would take her. She's not quite ready for the 110 yet so, we agreed on the fifty mile. Maybe the year after perhaps, you never know.

Cycling has improved my fitness and my stamina, I can easily get to work in less than thirty minutes now (my record is twenty-eight). I enjoy long rides with plenty of climbs, I just look at every ride as a challenge and one that I'm going to win! I have even tried the killer mile at Mow Cop, which is a VERY steep climb. I had looked at the record for the killer mile on Strava, which is a cycling app. The app shows you best times on different segments of roadway. The record was around five minutes, but it was only a mile.

It took me over twenty minutes to get up that one bloody hill, but I did it where many have failed. I'm going to do it again, and hopefully beat my own record. But I think the overall record is safe for now.

Cycling has made me fitter, faster and stronger, (up yours MS!) It also creates a good social life, meeting others as I have done. Making new friends and meeting other cyclists, who just seem to enjoy sharing experiences? They all seem very friendly. Coffee stops are a must. It's a lot better than social media sites, and more personal.

At the end of the day even illness doesn't have to hold you back. You can take over it, before it takes over you by getting on yer bike!

3. The Story .... So Far

Zara Bailey

I have been a competitive swimmer from the age of 8. Nearing the end of my being a competitive swimmer, I started thinking of new things, new challenges that would give me a buzz and let me see the fun side of doing sport. At the age of 14 I decided that since I used to be a county runner and I am okay on the bike so why don't I do it all and go into triathlons and see how I would find it. I struggled a lot academically and realising that I am a hands-on learner I left my mainstream school and started at JCB Academy as my dream job was to be a commercial pilot.

Dreams are short lived though. In May 2014 I started losing weight and lost a complete appetite for any food, as it always made me feel ill. Gradually I found myself fighting for breath even walking up the stairs I would have to sit down and take a minute. Due to the lack of oxygen and energy from not eating, every time I stood up, rooms would spin and I wouldn't be able to see, most of the time I would either fall over with lack of breath or because I couldn't think straight. All through this time I was saying "Never give up Zara, you can fight this, just take a deep breath and take a minute." I continued running, swimming and biking even though every time it became a very hard fight to just stand up. I couldn't stop half way through I needed to finish what I had started.

Walking into school was harder than it all because I couldn't pay attention, nothing was staying in my head long enough to write notes. Slowly my work deteriorated and so did my health. I started falling asleep in lessons and would sleep from the moment I got out of school to the moment I got to running. I would do the session struggling so much for breath I would always be stopping. As soon as the session finished I would get in the car and fall back to sleep. Throughout this whole time I was going back and forth to the doctors every time I would know what they would say, “It is a virus it will sort itself out eventually.”

Days went into weeks and weeks went into months however they all became somewhat a blur to me. I was just noticing the dramatic change in my appearance. My hair was lank and dull when at one point it was full of life and looked healthy. Brown pigmentation began to spread up my arms and making its way down my body and up my legs. One day I woke up and realised that my menstrual cycle had become very irregular and then they had just stopped.

My Mum took me down to the doctor - by this time I couldn’t see the point because they were just going to say the same things over to me again. They took some blood tests and couldn’t see anything wrong apart from having a low white cell count and when I asked about my menstrual cycle they said sometimes these things happen but it should sort itself out in time.

August 2014, I had completely given up on caring about my personal appearance; my hair was lank and very thin, my face was gaunt and withdrawn with black bags under my eyes that would never disappear and I could no longer fit in size six clothing because I was that thin everything just hung off me. I hated everything about myself because I didn’t know what was wrong with me, I just wanted to be normal. I couldn’t remember the last time I had a good training session, because at this point I struggled to cope whilst I was lying down.

September 2014, I did the Inter-club Aquathlon, representing Newcastle Triathlon Club. I came 3rd out of the water even though I struggled a lot more than I normally do in swimming. Then I went on to the run, from the very start I couldn’t breathe or think and my vision had gone hazy. On the way back on the run I wasn’t coping very well at all my health was deteriorating fast and I didn’t even know what was happening around me.

After a while my coaches started to worry about where I was so one of them came out to check up on me and she found me collapsed. She said to me, "Zara, you need to stop." Instead I climbed back up to my feet whilst every muscle and every bone was weighing me down. I started to put one foot in front of the other and jogged to the finish line. My heart felt as if it no longer belonged to myself. At the finish line, I fell to the ground everything wouldn't stop spinning and I was so out of breath. Never-the-less, I finished that race. I would have never give up and let my team down.

From that day on my health just got worse.

By the end of October I was been taken to the doctors every other day, and yet they were still saying I had a virus. On the 26th October my Mum and Dad thought it would be best if I got out of the house and they would take me to get some fresh air around Stafford.

All the way round in every shop I had to stop and sit down on the floor. My head was in my hands I was in so much pain I couldn't see; rooms were spinning, but at that point something new occurred I could now see spots in my vision that I had never seen before. I was so out of breath and I felt so unfit and I couldn't take standing up anymore.

Whatever it was making me feel like this, it was finally beating me.

Yet again we made another trip to the doctors. However this time I was to see a different doctor. He checked my blood pressure when I sat down and said it was fine. I found the energy from somewhere to say that "It's not when I'm sat down it's when I am stood up." Yet again he checked my blood pressure but this time when I was stood up. I saw his facial expression change dramatically my blood pressure was exceptionally low. He said that I should not have been able to stand but like I say I am a fighter.

He got me to sit down again and took his stethoscope from around his neck to listen to my heart-beat. His facial expression changed yet again, he couldn't put it into words but I remember it clearly as if I was being told it now. "Your heart sounds as if I have a pillow between the stethoscope and my heart, I think you might have fluid round your heart."

I was rushed into hospital straight into the intensive care unit where no one really knew what was going on. Lots of blood tests and scans were carried out. I was attached to heart machines and had a drip. Five long days later I met my consultant who had been looking at all of my tests and she thought I might I have this illness called Addison's Disease*; however she wasn't certain.

She said to me she was going to carry out one last test to see if my kidneys were making any adrenaline at all. When the results came back I had a complete flat line of adrenaline so that made my illness come to light. When I was told that I would have this illness for life, I was distraught I knew I couldn't do any of the things I had planned. I definitely could no longer be a pilot.

Like I say dreams are short-lived, but it means others can come up and change your whole future. I cried for what seemed like ages but I can remember thinking this is it, I can't do it anymore it's too hard. It took months for my tablets to be on a reasonable dose, but I was still tired all the time and not back to myself and this meant I was struggling with school work.

School didn't understand my illness and they had to arrange a meeting with my consultant which took a very long time, as I now needed carers in school, just in case I ever collapsed, and they would know what to do. I missed nearly three months maybe more of my GCSE year. I was told by my head-teacher I had missed too much to carry on with as many subjects as I was doing so I dropped four of them. As it came closer to the time of my exams I was doing everything I could to try and catch up with what I had missed. Remembering I was still ill and had to do little bits at a time because I would be getting very tired very quickly. I started by going back to school and doing half days and then coming home to get some rest and when I was able to focus I would start doing work and revision at home because my main priority was catching up with everything.

The exam period began and I was allowed to take energy drinks and sweets in my exams so that I could have a sugar boost if I felt tired. When results day finally came I managed to come out with eight GCSE's in total and my family was so proud of me because I had had such a hard year with the amount of pressure I was under when I finally came out of hospital.

I was starting to get back into my training slowly, because I couldn't bear not been able to do all the sport I have always done from day one. When I don't do sport it is like something is missing, so I knew I had to get back into it and I was going to train as hard as I possibly could. I had decided that I really want to be a triathlete and if I put my mind to it then I could achieve that dream all I need to do is work hard and I'll get there.

I was still trying to find out all of the right doses that I needed, to keep my body systems level, but that didn't stop me. The winter came, along with the hard work. I joined in Watt* biking with the club and I came on so much because by the end of all the session I had knocked off a big chunk of time which meant I was one step closer to my goal.

I have now gone on to Newcastle College and I am studying health and social care level 3. It is hard work but I love it and now because of my illness I have found a new dream a dream of becoming a paediatric nurse and going to Keele University. I have finished my first year there and came out with two distinction stars which I never thought I could do. On the 7th September 2016 I am going back to college to finish my second year and I am hoping to come out with the highest grade of three distinction stars.

This last year just gone I have done six triathlons. Starting with Wombourne Triathlon and finishing with Hever Castle Triathlon. Throughout the whole year I have slowly progressed and I have been coming in the top ten, which has given me the incentive to train even harder throughout this coming winter. Triathlons have become like a drug to me, as soon as I have finished one I want to get straight back in and do it all again. I have never experienced a buzz like it before and I don't think I will ever be able to replace it.

However I cannot put into words just how grateful I am for have two amazing coaches and two very supportive parents that have all driven me to try my hardest and to do my best. Even when I am low my Mum will make me realise that I can chase my dreams and nothing can stop me.

There are three particular adults in the club that have gone out of their way to look after me, support me and train with me. Also there is one person of similar age to myself who has been outstanding, supportive and always there. I could never thank these people enough for what they have done and what they are still doing today.

Throughout this whole time my Mum is the main person to thank because without her I would be dead; she was the only one who knew I was ill and the only one who insisted that I needed to be seen by a doctor. Mum has supported me through so much taking me to and from triathlons, helping me with revision through my exams and just been a fantastic mum she does so much for me she is like no one else I have ever met.

This is my story and I have written it to let people out there know that whatever you're fighting whatever illness you have you can fight to achieve your goals. It won't be easy but in the end it all pays off and there will always be hope because you only have to look at the people in the Paralympics to give you the inspiration you need.

* Addison's Disease: A condition caused by the failure of the adrenal glands to produce sufficient or any vital hormones.

* Watt Bike: a static bicycle with digital ability to measure performance and support training plans.

Captions. Top: this was before I was diagnosed. When I looked back on these two photos they scared me because I was that thin I look like a skeleton, Bottom: 19 months later, these photos have been taken throughout this past year and as you can see there is a dramatic change is appearance. I look healthier now and happier.

4. My Dream

Jessica Barnhouse

Jessica is one of five pupils from St Joseph's College with a stirring sporting story in this book. Read hers below; Sophie Longmore's on p.158; Gianni Loska's on p.160; Ilenia Sims' on p.192; and David Tierney's on p.209. Between them they cover swimming, sailing, triathlon, cricket and ball sports – a great mix.

Was this my time to shine? Was this my once in a life-time opportunity? Anxious, nervous, frightened, I sat bolt upright in bed thinking of all the terrible swimming races I have swum in the past! "Take your marks".... GO, I hate, absolutely hate these three words! Unfortunately, I seem to mess up every race I do!

Tuesday 15th September

5.00am: up bright and early for swimming training, practising and training my very best. I will not give up, one day I will succeed! Anxiously, I wait on the diving block, I hear those dreadful three words: "take your marks"... go! I swim my very fastest, I touch the end of the pool: I just got my personal best! Although this was only a swimming practice, I am very proud of myself! Only three more days to my big swimming competition.

Wednesday 16th September

8:00pm: back training at the swimming pool for the last time before my competition. Swimming, kicking, pulling, I am training my absolute hardest. I am being the best in this competition and nothing is going to stop me!

Race day!

The day has finally come! All kinds of feelings are buzzing around me: nervous, excited, anxious and certainly frightened! It is a long and nervous wait until my race. Sitting in the same old seat for two hours! One hour gone... getting nervous... another hour gone... feeling absolutely petrified!

I stand nervously on the diving block! All I can think of is myself right now, nobody else! The horn goes, I get ready, those three dreadful words I now hear, "take your marks"... go! I dive out into the distance, kick and pull as hard as possible, I am slowly but definitely making my way to first place. I am doing the best ever, I might actually make it! 15m from the end, I am going full out! Kicking as fast as possible, tiring my arms out, I think I've honestly done it! My hand touches the wall with anticipation, I've come 1st, hello people, I just came 1st. I cannot believe it.

So remember, never, ever give up on any of your dreams, even if they seem impossible to reach!

5. The Race of Truth: Riding the Mersey Roads 24 Hour TT

Andy Barratt

It's almost comical how one seems to forget the aching muscles, the coldness and the tiredness that the 24-hour Time Trial places on your body. This year was very much the same with little warmth from the sun, which had selfishly decided to ration itself to a bare minimum. Quina Brook circuit was a wash out, with a sign saying road closed due to flooding. Mersey Roads Cycling Club had decided to use the Preece-Espley-Preece circuit. I didn't mind, in fact just the thought of that ruddy great hill on the Battlefield stretch was a bit daunting.

Alan Purchase, a founder member of the Kidsgrove Wheelers looked set for the task in hand, in fact from where I was standing he looked better prepared than myself. Alan is a bit of a mile muncher, riding Manchester airport and back to Stoke two to three times a week just for the love of cycling.

As we approached the start line a lone piper played his bagpipes to each rider that passed by, there is something about bagpipes that send a shiver down my spine whenever played. Spirits were amazingly high despite the rotten weather. 5-4-3-2-1 - I'm off. The first six hours I found myself constantly changing my wet weather jacket, on, off, on, off, it was bloody annoying to say the least.

For the first 100 miles I couldn't seem to get comfortable in my tri-bars and my back was beginning to ache, so I decided to change my bike for the remainder of the race. When looking back it was a wise decision. I saw my team mate Alan several times as we passed and exchanged a friendly wave to one another.

The darkness slowly started to draw in and I pulled into Preece Heath and collected my lights from family members Pauline and Barry. At Preece roundabout there were lots of people shouting encouragement, which is always great to see every year. As I always say, ”A shout of encouragement is worth five miles or more in my book”. All our friends, family and club members had turned out in the awful weather to give Alan and myself a shout and to help us out. It made me feel very proud and humble, to say the very least.

190 miles had passed by on my speedometer and I felt it time to pull in on Espley Island and have a well-deserved brew and a sleep in the back of my friend Mark Harrison’s van. Just as I was dozing off I heard a voice I recognised, it was Alan, he had just pulled up for a brew, when asked how he was feeling he said,” I feel good”. I knew Alan was going to make it, as he said on one club night, “I will finish the 24 Hour, regardless”.

As I pushed on through the night and into the early hours of the morning I decided to take my third change of clothing as I was soaked to the skin yet again, a mixture of rain and sweat. Just before I did so I felt myself slipping into a bad patch, feeling sick and slightly dizzy - due to forgetting to drink from my water bottle, just before Espley Island? I wasn’t sure if I needed to be sick, or run to the loo. Either way I knew I was in trouble. I had pulled over, unclipped and slumped my head into my hands that were resting on my handlebars. I had a breather and just hoped that my wife Angie and friend Mark were at Espley Island and not Preece Island as was planned. I rode a few more miles and finally made it to Espley Island and there they were with a brew ready for me, I can’t tell you how thankful I was. I had a bowl of soup and drank my brew and felt like someone had given me a new set of legs.

The morning had broken and Alan and I were directed to the finishing circuit at the same time. By this time I had clocked approximately 285 miles and to push for my PB of 332 miles I knew I had to do something special. In the state that I was in with only three and a half hours to go it was looking like a PB might just be possible. I had a tin of Red Bull and a chocolate bar and gave it everything my legs had left to give. I finally made it to the

finishing circuit and raced around the twisty slippery bends trying to notch up the mileage, bit by bit. I looked at my speedo and it was reading 325 miles with only a few minutes left to go, my PB was slipping away, and so was my strength.

Roy and Joan came past me several times in the car shouting and applauding - along with family members Angie, Barry and Pauline. Adrian Humpage from Stone Wheelers Cycling Club was at the very top of a hill, so he didn't see my good side as I got to the top. Club members Chris Patterson and Mark had cycled out from Stoke to watch Alan and myself on the finishing circuit. There were simply loads of cyclists and non-cyclists giving masses of support. I crossed my final timekeeper to finish in exactly the same spot as the previous year with a provisional distance of 327 miles, in 53rd position. Alan notched up a very respectable first time 24 Hour mileage of 238.71 miles and ended up in 68th position.

The race of truth...

6. Charlie and the Karvan go to… Middleport Park

Peter Hooper

A few words of explanation might be needed here. Part of the *Sporting Stories* project is to engage with new writers by running writing workshops at various events. It's a lot of fun – pitching up with some suitable facilities, encouraging potential writers to drop by and write about sport, or tell us a bit about their sporting life.

The first time we tried this was at the Potters 'Arf in June 2016, where we borrowed a large van with an awning from the City of Sport team at the City Council. 'We' in this case was me (Cox Bank Publishing), Giovanni Esposito (aka Spoz, performance poet, former poet laureate of Birmingham and former poet-in-residence of Birmingham City FC), Emma Dawson Varughese (founder of WorldLits and owner of a caravan-based 'world view' writing and literature workshop business), and Lotta Bowers of the City of Sport team and her daughter Emelia.

The idea was to get Potters 'Arf runners and spectators to drop in and write a bit about their participation in the event. Since the Potters 'Arf coincided with Stoke-on-Trent's Hot Air Literacy Festival, we also persuaded the Festival organisers to let us badge the workshop as an official Hot Air fringe event – we think the first time that a half marathon has doubled as a literary fringe event!

We learnt a lot from this experiment:

- Emma ran a small survey of spectators and runners in the city centre and discovered loads of enthusiasm to write, but the enthusiasm didn't always translate into writing.

- Having a poet-in-residence didn't lead to people queuing up to write poetry, but Spoz dealt with this by turning the workshop into a 'poetry takeaway' (Google it) which worked brilliantly – we got some really nice pieces based on conversations with runners.

- Lotta, aided by Emelia, made a big difference by being a sweeper and general helper on the day – a spare pair of hands really helps.
- Torrential rain before the race start and after the race finish, combined with a small awning, does not make for a busy workshop.
- Having the workshop organiser absent for most of the event (I was running the Potters 'Arf) may not have helped, except in garnering some credibility with the other runners.

Despite all the above, we had a great time - and post-event got enough stories to be able to produce the first Potters 'Arf book: *The Potters 'Arf 2016 – a Celebration of the Race*.

And so to Middleport. The community group Middleport Matters - and their force-of-nature that is Amelia Bilson - were organising a summer community festival in Middleport Park, in conjunction with the City of Sport team. With their encouragement we offered to pitch up and do a writing workshop on the day – Saturday 13th August. This time I was able to use Emma's caravan – the wonderful Karvan – and we had space to put up Emma's gazebo as well. Together with a random collection of camping, picnic and garden furniture we had an eye-catching and spacious workshop set-up. No poet this time, but Emma had introduced me to Charlie Walker, a local artist specialising in portraits, who we thought might capture some of our writers as they wrote. Charlie wasn't available for the whole day but agreed to pop by at some point to get a sense of what he might do at future workshops.

I scouted the venue out a few days in advance, when there was a smaller community event taking place, and picked what I thought would be a good spot to pull the Karvan onto, near to the cluster of marquees and gazebos at one end of the park, without having to take the Karvan across the park itself.

On the day of the event itself I turned up bright and early, to find that the heart of the activity and main attractions were on the other side of the field! The Karvan sat at one end, behind a slight rise, like some unwanted outcast from the main party. A quick consultation with Emma and we agreed to relocate to a strategically perfect spot between the takeaway van (of which more later) and Sporting Communities' people-magnet of fun games and competitions. The weather looked set fine and once we were repositioned I started to realise what a great draw the Karvan and the gazebo were. People who wanted to sit in the quiet and comfort of the Karvan, with no distractions, could do that. And others, who wanted to chill out on the carpets and cushions under the gazebo and sketch and draw, could do that instead.

It was heart-warming to see the gazebo completely full of families, all busy working away on lovely pieces of creativity. I hadn't quite envisaged quite so many small people engaging in the project, so it was wonderful see loads of little ones with their mums all completely engrossed in their work. Emma was brilliant with them, from her experience of working with schools, and we got some great stories and drawings. Charlie turned up mid-morning and ended up staying for ages, tucked away in the Karvan and sketching people while he chatted to them.

With Emma mostly in the gazebo and Charlie holding fort in the Karvan, I shuttled between the two and made frequent excursions around the other attractions to drum up business, with some success. It was good to chat to our neighbours Ben and Ross of Sporting Communities about their work with local communities, although I had enormous van-envy of their huge and wonderfully equipped 'van' (the size of a house) which looked to have great potential as an alternative workshop venue. Come mid-afternoon the crowds had thinned out a bit and I was able to catch up again with Amelia – and agree what a great event this had been. And more importantly, what a great community there is in Middleport, with some lovely stories. And here are some of our favourites from the day, starting with Meg's wonderful dancing poem.

Meg's parents were running the takeaway stand next to us and we were delighted when Meg set up camp with us in the gazebo. She was as bright as a button, full of enthusiasm and sat and worked with Emma on her poem for a good part of the afternoon. So in the end, despite not having Spoz with us, we still ended up a with a poetry takeaway!

My Dancing Poem – Meg Higgins

My dancing dream
Is to be in a good team
And make my dancing clean
And to be in a professional ballet team
Another one of my dreams is never to be mean
I was always energetic as a child
When I dance I have a big smile
I am very very wild
The way to succeed is to try

See page 109 for Meg's poem in its full glory.

Running – Sara Morris

One day a lady was poorly. She stayed in her home. Her family's love surrounded her and she began to feel better. The doctors and nurses visited her. They gave her small blue tablets. They tasted horrible and made her cry. Still, her family's love kept her strong. Eventually she began to feel better. Her jeans were tight but she walked again. Her walking stick was put away. She walked, a lot. She missed the outdoors and watching her children play.

She began to feel stronger and her jeans a little looser. Running after her energetic children she saw how well they looked. Their rosy red cheeks and long hair blowing. She needed to feel like them. She wanted to run. Her family worried. Still she wanted to run. The doctors and nurses "ummed" and "arred". Still told them she wanted to run. The day was blue and bright. She laced up her trainers. She ran. Each day she ran a little more. With each run she felt better than before. Her jeans were thrown away. Running made her feel normal. Made her family feel proud. Running had made her healthy and strong. Still she runs.

<u>Roller-skating - Penny Morris, Sara's older daughter</u>

Rammed my head on the dining table
Over and over I bash
Laughing as I get up
Laughing so much
Even when I bash my bottom
Rammed all over my leg

<u>Roller-skating – Eadie Morris, Sara's younger daughter</u>

I was roller-skating.
It makes me feel like I'm flying.
I go faster than a shooting star.
My roller-skates are my favourite colour, pink.

Father and daughter – Marvin Molloy

As a youngster I was football mad and as I was going in to under 16's I decided to leave my football team which I had played for, for many years amongst all my school friends. The team I left for was in the same league and it meant competing against all my mates.

At the end of the season we had both reached the cup final at Northwood Stadium, it had been built up and talked about at school for weeks.

The game came and it was tight and tense and finished 1-1 after extra time, which meant penalties. 1-1, 2-2, 3-3, 4-4 and then they missed their fifth penalty, it hit the crossbar, I was up next to take what could be the winner, their keeper knew me and he knew where I preferred to hit them… But it didn't matter, it went into the side of his net. 5-4 and the crowd went wild… champions, relief it was over and memorable times!

Maddison Taia Molloy

Once I was in school and we were playing basketball at dinner time and after we ate the teams switched sides, but I didn't know so every time I had the ball I ran towards our goal. All of my friends started to shout my name and I didn't even think about it until my friend came up to me and told me to go the other way, it was so funny.

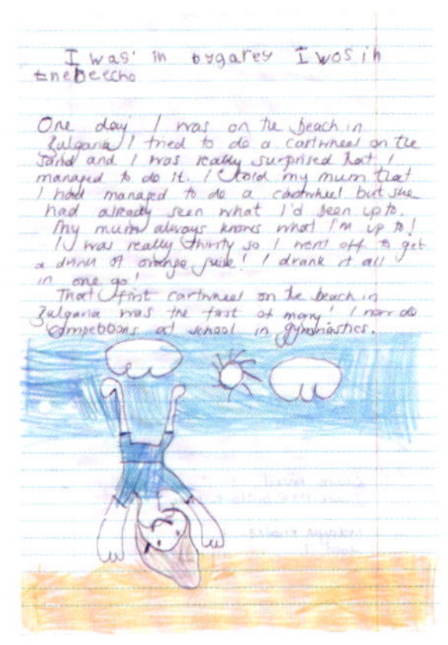
I was' in bygarey I wos in thebeecho

One day I was on the beach in Bulgaria I tried to do a cartwheel on the sand and I was really surprised that I managed to do it. I told my mum that I had managed to do a cartwheel but she had already seen what I'd been up to. My mum always knows what I'm up to! I was really thirsty so I went off to get a drink of orange juice! I drank it all in one go!
That first cartwheel on the beach in Bulgaria was the first of many! I now do competions at school in gymnastics.

Cartwheels - Mackayla Rhodes, 7

One day I was on the beach in Bulgaria. I tried to do a cartwheel on the sand and I was really surprised that I managed to do it.

I told my mum that I had managed to do a cartwheel, but she had already seen what I'd been up to. My mum always knows what I'm up to! I was really thirsty so I went off to get a drink of orange juice, I drank it all in one go!

That first cartwheel on the beach in Bulgaria was the first of many. I now do competitions at school in gymnastics.

Ice-skating - Gemma Woodworth

Ice-skating... the story of a lady needing to learn a new skill,
So ice-skating she thought, her time would fill,
Every Saturday trying not to fall or sink,
Upon the ice of the very slippery rink.
More and more techniques she did learn to do.
The competition was tough but the winner... who?
It's all about the learning, not about the win. It's a very good lesson needs passing to all.

Sienna-Ray Bryan, Lucie Woodworth and Gemma Woodworth proudly showing off their Sporting Stories

Mountain Biking - Amy Merry

A summer day in 2014, my aunt phoned with the offer of two mountain bikes. My daughter had recently learned to ride a bike so my first reaction was, a mountain bike – great for a family day out. So the deal was done – every Monday, my aunt and I set out on the Biddulph Valley Trail. The first time we went I certainly say it was horrendous. No enjoyment during the bike ride however by the end of the 13 mile ride I was exhausted and yet really pleased at the sense of achievement.

It got easier with each week, and the 13 miles actually became manageable. I feel much fitter these days and the mountain bike activity that I do makes me think that I would consider other sports that previously I wouldn't. These days we go further out such as The Tissington trail. I love the outdoors as part of the biking – we even go out in the rain!

Ice-skating - Karen Firkins

The cold overwhelmed me as I stepped out onto the ice rink. Scared, uncertain, heart pounding; why did I enter this competition? My feet feel chunky in the boots as I cling to the side of the rink. Never before have I stood on the ice. My tutor encourages everyone to let go of the side and attempt the warm up.

The cold is soon forgotten as my heart races, holding my body stiff trying not to fall over. I stomp with my right foot, then my left. Able to swing my arms and can't believe I'm still upright! Confidence building, could this actually be my new hobby?

Able to complete the warm up and skate (stomp) to the other side. Body finally relaxing and I was beginning to believe in myself more. Maybe there's hope for the Olympic dream after all.

Roller-skating - Tia Firkins (Karen's daughter)

Swishing side to side
Flying quickly down the road
can I stop in time?

Heart pounding quickly
flying down the road ahead
closer and closer

My many feelings
flying around my head freely
as the wheels go around

I get home tired, hungry
gasping for my quick, dear breath
walking up to home.

Trampolining - Chloe Tams, 10

There was a young girl called Hayley who had a passion for trampolining. She had blonde, wavy hair and eyes that shone in the moonlight. She wore blue, denim jeans with a red top. One day Hayley went trampolining and practiced for a competition. She tried and tried and all of a sudden she fell off the trampoline. Then a girl called Maddie told her "If you do that at a competition, you get laughed at by everybody". Sooner or later Hayley went home; she was so upset. The next day of school, her best friend said to her "Don't worry as long as you believe". A few days later at the competition, she did her amazing routine and got a gold medal! Her face lit up brighter than the sky.

Football – Emmett, 4

Sports is a great thing, when my age was three I played football. Sport has lots of balls.

7. My Cat & Fiddle Challenge

Erin Boddice

Erin is a member of Wyre Forest CRC, predominantly racing and riding her bike on the competitive circuit, but she enjoys riding cyclocross through the winter to keep her fitness up during the road off-season. She is a nationally ranked rider for both cyclocross and circuit racing. 2015 was her first year of racing: she finished third in her first regional event.

In 2016 she completed her first full season of racing and finished third in the West Midlands Youth League. She has now been put onto the Great Britain Cycling Regional School of Racing. The next step on the Team GB Rider Route is the Olympic Development Academy.

She decided to ride the Cat and Fiddle challenge because she wanted to support Cystic Fibrosis Care and enjoy a challenging ride with her family. The Cat and Fiddle Challenge is the longest and hilliest ride she's ever done – what a great one to start with!

The Challenge

It was 6AM on the morning of Sunday the 16th of October and we woke up to a cloudless black sky, littered with glistening, polar-white stars. Reluctantly, but remembering the worthwhile cause of this ride, I dragged myself out of my bed and put on just about every item of winter cycling kit I own!

My mum, my dad and I drove to a neighbouring town to pick up my cycling buddy and bacon sandwich provider, Craig. Sure enough the bacon sandwich was ready to go, wrapped in tinfoil and generously topped with ketchup! We continued our journey towards Stoke, the closer we got the greyer the sky became and the thicker the blanket of cloud grew. Then, the absolute biggest cycling nightmare came true… the heavens opened.

We arrived in Stoke and the rain was beating down on the car windows. We fastened our helmets, zipped up our rain rackets, clipped into our pedals and delivered the first pedal stroke. There was no going back now! We battled the rain with unresponsive breaks, dodging every manhole cover, because they had become a one-way ticket to sliding across the tarmac! We had a few difficulties finding the start and ended up climbing a few more hills than necessary!

The route was fantastic and we all rode brilliantly as a team, passing slower riders left right and centre. Clear skies were a welcome sight and when the rain subsided, we all breathed a sigh of relief! It was going brilliantly until we got to 'that hill'. We reached the Cat and Fiddle Climb at 25 miles in. I'm an absolutely rubbish climber, and despite being able to talk and breathe with... ease? my legs just wouldn't put the power through the pedals. Craig and my mum rode ahead, haha, thanks guys! Luckily my dad stayed with me, offering words of encouragement and motivation. My legs felt like jelly and every time I thought we had reached the top, there was yet another climb. I managed to force a smile; come grimace for the photographer. It was such a relief to reach the Cat and Fiddle pub for a well-deserved drink and flapjack! We started what we believed to be our descent. Little did we realise there was more tough climbing to come.

We finally reached the summit of the climb. My dad tells me the views of the Peak District National Park were beautiful, but I was too scared I was going to be blown off my bike by the fierce cross-wind if my concentration lapsed for just a moment. We glided down the first 14% descent relieved that gravity was working with, not against us. The second descent was even faster at a 17% gradient we neared speeds of 40mph. We were 35 miles into the sportive and I could have quite easily stopped there.

I thought that the last 20 miles would be easier and we would have a flat run into the finish. I was wrong. The remaining distance was to be the hardest 20 miles I have done. The rolling hills were the last thing my dead legs needed. And when I really wanted to get off and walk, thankfully my dad was strong enough to give me a helping push up some of the last, sharpest hills. At 45 miles I had a mini meltdown, I was pushed over the edge by a barking Jack Russell, it might sound stupid but dogs are my biggest fear. When my breathing was already laboured the dog made my breaths very shallow and fast. And okay, yes, I started to cry. “I can’t do it” I said, my dad said I could. Well I did.

The finish line was a welcome sight, and I helped myself to not one, but two slices of homemade chocolate cake and a helping of mini sausage rolls. I was so happy that I did the ride, and on reflection, I did enjoy it!

55 miles ridden, 3,835ft climbed and 1,501 calories burnt!

8. Paralympic Journey

Jenny Booth

So the 2016 Olympics ended in glory for TeamGB, but if you thought that was inspirational, they were followed by the Rio Paralympics - featuring elite athletes who have overcome enormous challenges to be able to represent their country at the highest level. This is the story of local parathlete swimmer Jenny Booth, and her 1996 journey.

It's finally here the letter I've been waiting for!!! Dare I open it, will it have the news I want, I'm so excited, let me explain a little.......

Many years ago after a big operation on my spine I joined a swimming class it was actually with some pensioners but it was perfect I just wanted a gentle swim to get back some mobility. I'd started to get a little stronger and my swimming stroke was improving it was suggested I join a swimming club as I was not a bad swimmer. So many many years ago I joined COSACSS Swimming Club, I still train with them today now with Senior Coach Greg Clarke at Fenton Manor we are ready for training at 5:30am, but little did I know how things would turn out.... There were some great swimmers in the club if only I could swim as well as them in the future! I always remember the day I moved from the middle lane up to the top lane the fast lane wow I thought I'd made it then, but there was more to come.

I did my first competitions, they were very basic to begin with but I progressed and I moved on to Regional competitions and then the National Championships held in Darlington at the time, that was a big occasion, I felt really excited. From there I got picked to join the Great British Team, we used to go away on training weekends to Stoke Mandeville and

Sutton Coldfield. They were really tough, we were up early and trained three swim sessions with lectures on nutrition etc and land training all fitted into busy weekends but they all stood me in good stead.

So back to the letter!

I was waiting to hear if I had been selected for the Paralympic Team to fly out to Atlanta to compete for GB again. I had competed at the Barcelona Paralympic Games which was a great honour for me, I swam personal best times in my races and made the finals. So the last four years of hard training and competing around the world at European and World Championships had all come down to the unopened letter I held in my hand!!!

YES...... I had been selected, the many hours of training and miles and miles I had swam had paid off, my name was on the list, I had earned a place on the GB Team. As time got closer my training sessions had been fine tuned for me to be at my peak for the games the kit had arrived and everything was coming together.

The team flew out to a holding camp in Pensacola Florida before the games so we could all acclimatise and put final preparations into place, from there we flew on to Atlanta (what a massive airport) and then to the Paralympic Village. The Village is an amazing place there's nothing quite like it with almost 6,000 living there, competitors, team staff and coaches, plus officials covering 19 different sports from 104 competing countries. It's a very colourful busy bustling environment to be in there are flags everywhere with all the different cultures and nationalities connected by sport coming together in one place.

The Opening Ceremony

There was a lot of waiting around as all the teams gathered GB looked smart all dressed in our walking out uniform. It was time for our country to march into the Athletics Stadium the roar of the 66,000 strong crowd was so loud and when the Mexican Wave started going around it got even louder if that was at all possible. The talks and speeches were taking place with a very touching one from Christopher Reeves (yes Superman was right up there in front of me). The whole ceremony is a very loud, action packed exciting experience. The lighting of the Paralympic Flame is a poignant moment and always a little sad when it's extinguished nine days later.

Time to race

I had competed my individual races and made the finals, I had given it my all and recorded personal best times. The 4 x 50m Freestyle Relay team had been decided and announced and I had been chosen, amazing, but I was chosen to swim the last leg the anchor leg, so much pressure...... it felt like the whole result of the race was down to me. Over the last few years as part of the GB Relay Team we had had some tough battles against the strong French Team and it had all been a matter of which team swam best on the day.

The day of the relay, all competitors have to report to the call room to have final accreditation checks a little before the race, for those of you that have ever been in such a room you will know what I mean by it's a very strange place. Swimmers are trying to psych themselves up, others are trying to psych their competitors out some listen to music and others are stretching/warming up and there's always that familiar smell of muscle rub...... Pressure builds to boiling point then we get the go ahead to parade out to the pool.

I was extremely nervous but at the same time ready to race so nerves had to be set to one side we had a job to do. If ever I wanted to swim well it was today I had to have confidence that all the training I had done all the miles swam and the gym work, would all pay off. The French team had saved their fastest swimmer for the last leg, she had a lesser disability which meant she could dive and also had a leg kick, which I have neither. So the girls in our team knew they had to give me a lead or we didn't stand a chance, they did, we all swam our hearts out when I took over we were leading could I hold on to the lead. I heard the cheer of the almost 15,000 capacity crowd get louder which could only mean one thing she was chasing me down......

I hit the time pad right on the end of a stroke perfect, we had all done it and finished in first place yes **GOLD MEDAL** position was ours, not only that we had set a **NEW WORLD RECORD**. Wow we had now just become the four fastest swimmers with our disability classification in the world ever for this event!!!!!!!

A little while later after many photos and autograph signings and a few verses of "We are the Champions" and "Simply the Best" it was time for the Medal Presentation. With the National Anthem playing and the Union Jack on the flagpole we were there on the top of the Medal Podium and I think you could say on top of the world right then.

Returning home

I felt like a hero everyone wanted to hear about the trip and what it was like out there, Newspapers and Radio wanted interviews. I was invited to all kinds of events... I remember the first standing ovation I got, felt very special.

I won Stoke-on-Trent's overall Female Sports Personality of the year what a privilege to be awarded such a great title and to be presented with the trophy by Lou Macari and John Rudge, what a moment, very proud. I even got an invite to a Reception at Buckingham Palace I was to meet the Queen!!!

Still to this day I get invited to events, earlier this year I was a Heart Bearer at the Opening Ceremony for Stoke-on-Trent's 2016 European City of Sport celebration. There were many local sports stars there when you look around what great talent has come out of Stoke-on-Trent. I got chatting with many guests including Colin Jackson, Amy Williams and Jonathan Edwards, a great privilege for me and for Stoke-on-Trent.

It just goes to show we are never quite sure where the journey of life will take us, I never thought my swimming would have taken me all over the world from Stoke-on-Trent to America, Australia, New Zealand and many countries in between. If sport is included in our journey, it can only be a good thing.

Oh, I won a **BRONZE MEDAL** in Atlanta too, in the Medley Relay.......

9. The Sloth: The Roaches HVS 5a/b

Duncan Bourne

Writer, cartoonist, poet - Duncan Bourne brings it all to bear on his love of climbing. This is his account of a tricky climb in the Staffordshire Moorlands.

Head out of Leek along the A53 and you will see the Roaches dominating the skyline like a recumbent sleeping dragon, guarding the gateway to the Peak District. Generations of walkers and climbers have been drawn to explore the rugged gritstone scales of this slumbering giant rising from its nest of ancient, twisted pines and larch and I am no different. Countless times I have trudged the steep path to Rock Hall, an edifice half house half castle built into the very rock. Once occupied by the scarily eccentric "Doug", self-styled King of the Roaches, whose garden bristled with cheery signs saying things like "Trespassers will be shot!" and "This could be you so watch it!" hung round the chest of stuffed scarecrow hanging by its neck (these days it functions as a charming bunkhouse for weekend Londoners, its reputation tamed).

From Rock Hall I would follow the path up through the pines to a set of stone steps and climb steeply through the lower gritstone crags to the exposed Upper Tier. Here it was that my eyes were always drawn to the great overhang that dominates the main section of the crag and, snaking up through it, the single widening crack that forms "The Sloth". To me the Sloth had always been more than just a climb, it was THE Sloth, a climb symbolic of dead 'ard routes. True it's only HVS, a middling grade in the climbing world these days, and there are far harder more exposed routes around. But, when I started climbing, we would walk up to the Roaches glance at Valkyrie, on the lower tier, and think "maybe next year". Then mount the steps onto the upper tier and gaze up at that imposing roof and someone would say, "fancy Sloth?" Much along the same lines as someone saying, "do you fancy wrestling rabid crocodiles?" It was a joke, only the hard men climbed Sloth, there was no way that I ever could. But still I looked at it and thought wouldn't it be great.

So here I was, years later, trudging up to tackle something that I still considered scary, even though I now regularly climbed harder grades.

There was a stiff breeze blowing and I wondered if it would be too windy, a reprieve? Hopefully? No, the base of the crag was sheltered and there was my Nemesis, aloof and intimidating amidst the crowd of Outward Bound groups that top roped around it. I strode forward, claimed my spot and warmed up. I bouldered a little and found the friction excellent. Putting off the moment? Oh well time to go for it. I used double ropes and quickly climbed up to the Pedestal block where I placed my first runner in a thin crack. I looked at the roof stretching dark above me and the exposure hit me with cold sweat and an attack of “disco leg”. I rested a few moments to calm myself then I moved up and clipped the wire of an abandoned piece of gear jammed into the block overhead. Tentatively I tried the first of the creaking flakes, felt OK but boy was it a long way down! I placed a friend half in the crack and moved back down to the pedestal.

More calming exercises followed. Back up I went and moved further out, an upside down spider along the fragile seeming flakes of rock. Placing a quadcam 3.5 in a suitable hole, I hung there a moment then moved cautiously onward. With gravity pulling at me I hooked my feet into the horizontal flake and hooked a Hex 8 into a wide crack where the rock moved from the horizontal overhang into the merely vertical. No backing out now. With a pounding heart I pulled quickly round the lip, trying not to swing free as I did so, and squirmed quickly into the widening crack above, with a moment of panic as my nut key caught on the rock temporarily halting my progress. Then it was over. It felt weird to romp up that last upper crack, where I had gazed with awe at so many climbers in the past. It seemed like I had crossed over some personal threshold and achieved something I had once thought impossible.

So now when I visit the Roaches and someone says, jokingly, "Do you fancy Sloth?" I can reply, "Naa done it!"

10. Potteries Adventures

Tom Brennan

An important project for the Sporting Stories initiative in the summer of 2016 was a collaboration with Stoke City Football Club's Community Trust. The Community Trust works with the National Citizen Service to provide volunteering opportunities through the summer for groups of young people aged 15-17. One of the NCS cohorts asked to help Cox Bank Publishing to help collect local sporting stories. This particular cohort was on the NCS scheme for July, culminating in a final week spent working with the company and the Community Trust, visiting a range of community groups and care homes to interview people about their engagement in sport. The volunteers got a huge amount out of this and collected some really interesting stories, with the support of the Community Trust.

On top of these visits, we also arranged for the team to practice their interviewing and writing skills on a couple of local 'stars' with stories to tell, with support from Cox Bank Publishing, from Dave Proudlove, a local writer, and Stoke-on-Trent Sixth Form College student Rebecca Latham. Tom ('young' Tom), seconded to us for the morning from his day job at Go Outdoors, spoke about his climbing adventures; and former Lord Mayor and runner Tom Brennan spoke about his adventurous childhood. Some great stories from both, but it was Tom Brennan's stories of his youth, growing up in Burslem in the 1930s and '40s, that transfixed the group, so much so that they asked to meet Tom again to hear more and to produce a little ghost-written autobiography for him.

Thanks in particular to Georgia Oldham for taking the lead on writing Tom's story, with a supporting cast of Wendy Atsu, Andrea Beech, Ben Cross, Liam Hall, Tamar Kuma, Naomi Lehepuu, Lemar Mingo and Tom Simpson.

The Adventure Playground: A Potteries Childhood by Kate Ackley, reproduced with permission of the artist

Tom's story: A Potteries Childhood

When I was a boy in the 1930s, I grew up in Burslem living in extremely poor conditions, surrounded by factories and pollution. I was the oldest of five children in a religious Catholic family, which meant as I grew older, I was expected to show guidance to my younger brothers and sister. Although as a young boy with a taste for adventure I wasn't always setting the best example!

Because I was born into these tough conditions, I thought it was the norm and a part of everyday life, even though our streets were surrounded by mounds of rubbish, open mine shafts and dirty canals. It wasn't like living in a town - it was like living in a factory. The only day clear of smoke and pollution was Sunday, when the factories shut down. Children who were poorly were sent into the country for the clean air.

There was a lot of disease – polio, scarlet fever, measles, scabies – life was tough for everyone and you always knew of someone who was dying. I had only hand-me down clothes and clogs, no shoes. Clogs were perfect for skidding down rails and steep slopes though, and you could kick a ball miles with them.

I used to run errands for the family, and I ran everywhere, just for the love of it. School sports were on a rough bit of road behind the school, and I was already faster than anyone else. Running was in the family, my uncle Tom was a runner and played centre forward for Port Vale FC. There was no other encouragement for running from the community. Even back then I wondered why there weren't any sports facilities in the City.

It was extremely difficult to get away from the environment we were living in, so we had to make our own entertainment - this entertainment was the only recreation of young people at the time. I shudder to think now of the things we did – racing the train (in front of the train on the track), walking blindfold across planks over open pit shafts. The real test of manliness though was a two-mile swim, starting at Shelton Bar and going all the way down to Westport Lake.

Not only did we have to swim, but we also had to jump off different bridges throughout, and a very dangerous part of the challenge was to swim underneath the long barges that transferred goods down the canal. This was very hazardous and the people on the barges highly disapproved and threw planks of wood and other objects at us, but we enjoyed it. The canal was riddled with dirt and disease due to the local factories treating it as a dumping ground, but we didn't care because it was our only enjoyment and it was our paradise.

The swim proved our hardness and those who completed the "Doffer" were afforded great respect by their friends and the rest of the youth in the community. It was also a chance to prove that you belonged.

Another activity local children did was being a lookout for the men who played cards up on the 'burning banks' where coal seams were on fire. Gambling was not allowed and extremely frowned upon so the men who played it had to play it in private, using children as their lookout – you could earn a whole sixpence for this job, although I never did. We also used to take potatoes up to this bank to bake in the ground - these were a delicacy to us kids back then.

In 1947 there was a miners strike, and with no coal then finding fuel that winter was really important. I used to go exploring up Bradwell Wood and one day while collecting firewood up there I found a bit of brown coal – a small seam exposed in the bank. I collected a bit and took it home to show my Dad. The next day we went back with a bucket and collected more, but some other people saw us and the next day there were hundreds in the wood digging out the seam and after a few days the police came because they were worried some of the diggings might collapse and bury people.

On an earlier trip to the wood I'd seen an old pick at the bottom of a steep bank by an old clay pit. I took my dad there to show him and without thinking I jumped down to get the pick, to use it to get more brown coal. I hit the base of the slope but it was muddy and very slippery and I shot down into the water of the clay pit. I was buried up to my knees in silt and was pitching forward into the water. I don't know how but I managed to grab the pick and throw myself back and bury the pick's head in the bank above me. If it hadn't stuck in the ground I'm not sure what would have happened. I managed to pull myself out but not my precious wellies which were lost forever in the mud. I can't repeat what my dad said when I got back up to the top of the bank, and I had to walk a mile home in bare feet.

The 1947 winter was a really hard one and despite our adventures in gathering wood and coal it was hard to find enough fuel, especially when everyone was in the same situation. My youngest brother John caught gastroenteritis and simply wasn't able to fight it off. We lost him at only five months old. The memory of his tiny white coffin on my father's knees on the way to the funeral has never left me.

I left school at 14 to start work, for seven shillings and sixpence a week, which I gave to my mother. She instilled strong principles in us all. She used to say "Look all around you, not just in front of you", and "What can you find to better yourself? And to better other people's lives?". All of the sports and activities I did growing up in the '30s and '40s were based around my mother's morals and values that she had drummed into me throughout my early childhood. They have helped to mould me into the man I am today and influence the decisions I make in my day-to-day life. One thing I would advise all young people to do if they want something in life, is to stick to their ambitions. Once you show that you can stick to your goal, you are guaranteed to make a difference, not only to your life but importantly to your community as well.

Tom went on to become Lord Mayor of Stoke-on-Trent and was the driving force behind the construction of the international standard Northwood Athletics Stadium in the city. Read more about his life at www.sportingstories.com

11. Peter William Bunn, 72. It just had to be 72.

Anthony Bunn

This deeply personal story moved us to tears the first time we read it. Anthony Bunn's beautifully written eulogy on his father's love affair with Stoke City has been previously published elsewhere, including The Oatcake, but we're delighted to republish it here with Anthony's permission. Anthony is a freelance writer and the editor of DUCK magazine – which you should check out if you can: it's a (mostly) football magazine with bags of style and great writing. It's also a big supporter of the Donna Louise Trust. The image on p.72 (72 again) is taken from a DUCK cover.

"Unlike most football fans, I can't really remember my first Stoke game. My first clear memories of watching us were against Middlesbrough at Vale Park and then having a season ticket in 1977 in the Butler Street Stand. Relegation, inevitably, soon followed.

So, basically, I was introduced to the Potters after a visit to our local rivals ground, then being forced to sit in probably the only roofless sitting area in Britain at that time and watch us go down..........But am I grateful that my old man grasped my 8-year old hand all those years ago and walked me to those turnstiles? What a daft, rhetorical question."

Fathers are all too often the Nigel Gleghorn (or Glenn Whelan) of families – they do lots of unseen work that always needs doing; they rarely get the adoration they deserve; often steering the ship in the right direction; they have a quiet, unassuming style all of their own, and rarely let anyone down.

That was Peter William Bunn. And I will now always have the stomach-churning task of writing about him in a different tense.

Because dad sadly passed away on 24th November 2012, just an hour after watching the club he worshiped beat Fulham 1-0 at the Britannia Stadium. That he did so at around 5.45pm, just as Praise and Grumble was on, isn't just ironic, it's fate. Talking about Stoke City was one of life's joys for dad. He also loved listening to the post-match Radio Stoke show every week.

It's also fate, not irony, that he was aged 72 when he died. It simply couldn't be any other number, could it?

Add onto the fact that he went quickly, and relatively painlessly, to sleep on the shoulder of his very best mate Terry (my uncle, who was driving), and that they were within a Greenhoff volley or Sir Stan mazy dribble of the Victoria Ground, simply makes me smile and actually think that if Carlsberg did ways to pass away......

Perhaps I'm looking for fate when there's simply none there?

But whilst football is never ever "more than life or death", it gives me huge comfort that dad passed away on such a seamlessly brilliant Stoke City Saturday afternoon.

The analogy with Nigel Gleghorn was given careful thought. He was a player my father admired – a flashback to players who loved their football, with a wand of a left foot, and one who always seemed grateful to be playing the working man's ballet and to be playing for Stoke City. He also scored a most memorable goal in front of me and my father – no, not our second at Vale Park or against Plymouth at the Victoria Ground to seal the deal on promotion in 1993.

It involved another Victoria – this time it was Victoria Park, the home of Hartlepool United. It's one of my favourite awaydays of all time and dad can be vividly, easily seen on the telly on Central Sport a day or two later– to the right of the goal, jumping up and down as the 90th minute corner came in, not in anticipation of Gleghorn's late winner, but because his bladder was about to explode thanks to his pre-match refreshments, after an unbelievable Usain Bolt-like sprint from coach to public house at 2.25pm!

It had to be in that 92/93 season, didn't it? So many great memories, so many days when me, dad, Terry, Brad, Owen, Andy, Tim and a few others I can't remember right now, would descend on football grounds the country over, watching Lou Macari's team.

That day, for some reason, it was just me and dad. The 20th December 1992....... a dad and his son celebrating their team's last minute winner, together, on the road to promotion, stood on an open terrace. Heaven.

No-one was prouder of Stoke City or Stoke-on-Trent than Peter William Bunn. When on holiday, he'd nearly always be spotted in a Stoke sweatshirt or t-shirt; it was like a privilege, a badge of honour. He saw it as almost 'representing' his city and club in foreign climes. The Cultural Attaché for Sneyd Green.

I vividly remember Wembley in 2000, and after beating Bristol City 2-1, we giddily went back to Harrow-on-the-Hill where our buses were parked. We went into a huge pub, full of Arsenal fans watching their team's live game at Leeds. As we flooded into the pub, high on winning a trophy, no matter how small, we were given the usual *"big-club, northern idiots"* jibes from the deluded, self-admiring, self-loving Gunners, looking right down their noses at us as we entered.

Half an hour later, as the coaches were due to leave on the journey back to The Potteries. Dad had had enough.

"Sorry, but I'm not letting them run Stoke down. Back me up, lads", he announced. Then, as the assembled Stokies prepared to depart, and at the tender age of 60, he stood, arms outstretched on a chair, and shushed the pub before leading a huge, proud 'Delilah' that finally shut those of an Arsenal persuasion firmly up.

Although his Ashes are scattered at the Britannia Stadium – and by the way, the club were absolutely brilliant with the logistics of this – his heart and soul will forever remain with his family, and at the Victoria Ground.

Dad never really took to the Britannia Stadium.

For him, the lack of a 'proper' matchday routine had never really been replaced, even after 15 years at our new stadium. Dad's routine was drinking in the Gardeners Retreat or Michelin Club, both close to Campbell Road, and a five minute brisk stroll at 2.40pm to the ground: Campbell Road – Nicholls Street – Lime Street.

He loved holding court with tales of Sir Stan leaving the ball by the corner flag and his marker also leaving the ball and simply following him, or the time he kept a pub near Buxton from rioting at closing time as the assembled Stokies wanted to see the FA Cup semi final goals on the telly on their way back from Hillsborough.

I hope the tales he told were true, but if they weren't, we loved listening to them anyway: How he came back from Ajax so late that he and his mates simply went straight to Stoke's next game; or how he moved his wedding day to a Sunday to avoid a cricket match; and how he got a lift home on the team bus (and drank ale with the players) after his transport conked out on the way home from Spurs in the 70's (all of those are definitely true!). He told his tales time and again, but it didn't matter. Our group loved nursing a pint of 'Peddy' and watching the glint in his eye as he told them.

Proper Werther's Original stuff.

But strangely, what makes him unique is that he's just like any one of us.

Sounds daft that, yeah, but does anyone who **doesn't** follow their football club truly know what it means to belong to something so special? How can they ever replace taking their kid to watch their city's football club? How do they ever feel what we feel? Can their bond with their father ever be as emotionally watertight as ours is with our fathers who support the stripes?

I don't really know. I'm eternally grateful I don't.

All I do know is that me and my brother probably only now realise what we had and what we've lost, and that it would be a dream to be even half the dad he was, to our own kids. The hundreds of Stoke games we watched together and the hundreds of times he watched us, his lads, play football and cricket seem to have decreased in number as advancing years and grey hairs dim the memory. But deep down, we know he was always there, and now we somehow have to get used to the idea that he no longer is.

But isn't life also about what you leave behind?

If so, this proud man that me and my brother were honoured to call 'dad' has left something of more value than any lump sum of money ever could – he left us with the same standards as he had, a love of sport and the friendships this brings, to truly cherish our families, and that the North Wales sea is never too cold to swim in! He did so in a beautifully understated manner, too. He never moaned or shouted. Good men don't have to, do they? He was a true man of the Potteries, a proud Potteries man.

For me, my football club is such an integral part of who I am. That's why, at 12.01am November 25th 2012, – I wanted it to be the day **after** his death – I posted about my father's passing on The Oatcake Messageboard.

I still don't know truly why, to be honest, it's just that dad's family always seemed to include every single Stoke fan. The 11,000+ views and hundreds of messages meant more than anything to me and my family. Blokes who had been at games with dad in the '50s onwards contacted us; strangers who knew of dad and had funny stories emailed me; even Port Vale fans set up a thread on their own messageboard, which was a fantastic gesture. What it means, and this is so clichéd, I know, is that those who watch football really are one family. We feel what everyone else feels, we drink from the same cup, no matter the strip we wear. Whilst staunchly parochial, we all have a respect and give a knowing doff of the cap to those who go through the good and dreadful times following a football club.

Fenton Bowling Club – then watching Stoke win alongside his best mate – three generations of the Bunn's there at The Brit - going to sleep on his best mate – and 72, that beautiful, beautiful number, 72: It was scripted by the footballing Gods, dad, wasn't it?

Whilst it turns my stomach to know he's no longer here, it swells my heart to know that he went on his own terms and how many of us wouldn't want to go like that? I can't believe I won't see him in his SCFC manager's coat again, but he'll always be there, walking with us to the ground come sun, rain, snow, wind or whatever the weather throws at us. A truly wonderful Stokie.

That my dad got to walk down, well, shuffled down as he wasn't brilliant on his feet for some time, Wembley Way with his family on May 14th, 2011 now means everything to me. That we didn't win hurts, but it would have hurt more if we'd have won and he wasn't there!

Because even if we win the FA Cup one glorious day, it will never really mean the same without dad being present: standing still, huge beaming smile, and holding his arms high in the air when we scored, as he always did as utter carnage reigned around him.

Mere memories aren't enough, they never are. But they have to suffice as he's not here now. I pray he knew how much he was loved, but being a bloke I rarely said it enough when it was needed and necessary. I hope he could hear me as I stood by him, stroking his hair as he lay motionless, looking serenely at peace with the world, on that dreadful Saturday night at the hospital. "*We won dad, we won*", I kept muttering. He knew.

The final words?

They really do **have** to be from the most poignant, beautiful and apt football song ever written, don't they? A song that he actually sung on way back in 72, and one that simply sums up these 2012 (wow, fate again, eh?) words so well:

"We'll be with you every step along the way. We'll be with you, by your side we'll always stay."

Love you, dad. God bless.

12. The Golden Archers

Daniel Cartwright

Daniel is 12 years old and currently attends the Excel Academy. He wrote this piece while at Hillside Primary School, after a visit to Stanley Head Outdoor Education Centre.

He wanted to do archery since he was small. His mum found an open day event for a local archery club, the Six Towns Company of Archers, based at Werrington. Daniel went along to the event with his parents and had a go. He really enjoyed it, so he and his dad did the beginners course. When they had completed that they had a discussion and decided to become members. They now have their own bows, go every weekend, and have been doing archery for over a year now.

"Right archers you're with me wear a long sleeve top and meet at the staff room!" shouted the crazy Mr. Wilson. It was my group's time for archery and I was so excited. I do archery at the weekend at a school. I knew it wouldn't be the exact same because they are different clubs but I thought it wouldn't be much different - boy I was in for a shock! I sprinted at top speed down the path to the staff room, I couldn't be late. As carefully as I could, I swung round the corner doing a ninety degree spin. Once I got there (just in time) the worst thing happened it started to rain! We had no idea where we were going so we were dreading getting wet. Slowly but steadily we picked up the bows and walked down the steep, extra-long grass (I don't walk with a bow so that was new for me). Me and the other ten or so classmates tried to go fast to avoid the rain but we weren't allowed to run. It was going to be a soggy Wednesday afternoon! I was hoping that we would be in some sort of bunker for archery because I couldn't get my perfectly dry hair wet! Why did it have to rain on my favourite activity? We only wanted to do archery to learn about it.

Two minutes later, we made it. There were two shelters one with the targets in and one empty where you can shoot in. We put the bows on cut cones because it was the perfect stand for it. There was a snippet in the cone to put arrows. Usually I would have a proper stand to put it on. Mr. Wilson told us how to stand on the shooting line and not to go over it when other people are shooting. You could only cross it when everyone else had finished shooting. Then he told us how to load the bow and how to hold it. To hold it, you have to put your left arm where the slots are. To load it, he told us to turn it flat and slot the knock into the string underneath the golden circle (I would hold it normally then put the knock on the string not what he told us to do). After, Mr. Wilson said to put your middle three fingers under the arrow I was taught to use a finger guard where you put the index finger above the arrow and the one next to it finger underneath, your pinky on the rest and your thumb in the air. Finally he told us to pull it back as far as we could. Pull back so that the string is on the indent on my nose and my hand firmly under my chin. Once he'd showed us how to do it he had a go himself and he hit the centre of the target (a gold). He was really good. When it came to my turn I was really nervous. I was thinking, what if I do terrible? I'll be heartbroken.

I stepped up to the shooting line, did my technique, let go and- I hit the red! On my next go I did the same except I hit the gold! Finally, I hit the red again. My score was twenty-three out of thirty. I was so happy. Joyful, gleeful and amazed I collected my three arrows. After a few more practice shots, we gathered around and were given a number. I was given number one. The first game was race to the sun. you had to get the colours in order to win. You start with white, go to black, then to blue, after red it was finally gold. However, both teams were struggling, so after ten annoying minutes you didn't have to get them in order anymore. It was a lot easier then. It was tied four to four on colours; but you had to get the gold. Both teams were struggling to get it. Unfortunately, the opposition got it before the Golden Archers (my team was the Golden Archers.) The next game was bake a cake. I was used to this game because in my beginners course at archery we played it. We went up one colour; I got a blue. Sadly, we lost that game too! We started off in a good position with a flour, egg and water but we needed a red to get the cake cooked. The worst thing happened though - someone hit the black. It meant that the ingredients burnt and you had to start again. It gave the other team a huge advantage. As we had gotten our second colour we heard cheering from the other team; they had won. Their team was really good. Then we did an 'every man for themselves' contest on who could get the highest score. They now had four bows out so they went in fours to shoot. The scores were good for new people staring archery. When it came to my turn it was just me and Rebecca left to shoot. Once Rebecca had shot I was worried, it looked like she had a big score compared to mine.

When we went to collect I added up my score and had nineteen. What I didn't know was that Rebecca had the same. I went down to a 'first to hit the gold wins' contest. Unfortunately - for me - Rebecca hit the gold and I hit the blue. It was almost the end of the lesson when we had to do the challenge to hug a tree without touching the ground. As I thought - by thought I mean knew - I did terrible. Sam won out of our group with three minutes and fourteen seconds.

Once the session was over, I felt proud of what I had achieved. I was also looking forward to eating my tea with a knife and fork while people were dreading eating meat and potato pie with their hands because of the cutlery challenge. You had to eat your tea with (if you got the colours) white = drinking juice out of a bowl, black = having condiments, blue = knife, red = fork, and gold = spoon. I ended up with three forks. I did a few trades so I had a fork, knife and a bowl of juice to drink. I had really enjoyed the activity. The activity was full of fun, excitement and teamwork. Advice I would give would be: listen to instructors and don't be scared of any activity because they wouldn't let you do it if it wasn't safe.

13. My Journey

Lucas Christer

We're always keen to use images to illustrate the stories we publish and not just photos - paintings and drawings are always welcome. None more so than when the artwork is done by the author of the story - and we don't think any contributions are going to be better than this painting by Lucas Christer, and his description of it. Lucas plays Powerchair Football - the fastest growing disabled sport and due to become a Paralympic sport in 2024.

My name is Lucas Christer and I play powerchair football for St Georges Knights in the National League. I recently did a painting for Donna Louise Hospice which showed how my condition makes me feel. This is my journey. When you look into the sky at night and see the stars they just look like dots of light. When you look through a telescope you see the beauty of the universe and realise there is so much more. This is like me. When people look at me they see a boy in a wheelchair. You might feel sorry for me or just think there is nothing special. If you look closer and get to know me you realise there is so much more.

The painting represents how I feel at different times and the thoughts I have. There are dark spots where I think of not being able to walk anymore but the light behind is the good memories I have of when I could walk. Like doing the barefoot walk at Conkers. There are dark points where I think about always being stuck in my wheelchair but then the light parts are where I think about playing football and my dreams of playing for England. All the bad thoughts are equalled out by the good memories and the exciting things I have done because of my condition. I got to go to Florida with all my family and meet loads of new friends. I got to win the child of courage and meet famous people. There are bright parts showing my excitement at finishing runner up in the Stoke sports awards. I might be in a wheelchair but I am still a bright star.

14. Up For The Challenge: From The Start

Jeremy Cliffe

Earlier in the summer my brother and I travelled over to Nottingham to take part in the first of this year's British Nordic Walking Challenge Events. The event was set in the leafy suburbs, at the 500 hundred acre Wollaton Deer Park, with a spectacular backdrop of an Elizabethan Mansion Hall (which was actually used as a setting in the 2012 Batman Film – Dark Knight Rises).

Being relatively new to Nordic walking and being in our late 40's/early 50's we were slightly apprehensive, but thought we'd give it a go. As this was our first major Nordic walking event, we opted to take part in the 5km walk event (as we didn't feel quite ready for the half marathon just yet!). This was a very well organised event, and judging by the race numbers allocated for our shirts, we estimate that there were in the region of 250 walkers who took part overall in the 3 events – 5km, 10km and 21km (half marathon) – and surprisingly enough there were lots of people up for the challenge, much younger and much older than us!

After a quick warm-up session, the distance walkers went first, setting off in small groups, with a staggered start. It's quite difficult to know exactly how well you are doing in the overall race, which nicely takes the pressure and competitive edge off the event. In all honesty it didn't seem overly competitive, with most walkers just keen to beat their own previous time from the last event – and in fairness most of them did! There was loads of encouragement and support from the marshals and fellow competitors alike. To top it all the weather was just great, sunshine all the way, but not too hot for the walking!

A Walk In The Park: To The Finish

I led our group most of the way around the park, but perhaps went off a bit too quickly and got pipped at the post by my brother and another competitor, with shall we say, a rather interesting walking style and a pretty unconventional technique. We ended up second and third in our group and in the overall men's 5km event when the timings were collated. Not bad for a couple of 'owd Stokies' in our first challenge and being relatively new to the sport ourselves.

In fact it would be great to get a full team of four together for an event in the near future – who knows we might even win? Oh sorry, I forgot, we weren't supposed to be getting too competitive now were we!

Anyway well done to all who took part, and to those organising and marshalling too – and see you all next time around!

15. A Sporting Life

Viv Cotton

Viv Cotton is a life-long Stoke supporter and one of several residents from West End Village who have contributed to the Sporting Stories project. It's great to be able to share her story with a wider audience – and to read her memories alongside those of Ron Hughes (page 118) who has very similar recollections of the great Stoke players of the past.

When I was nine and at primary school, my dad took me to my first football match at the Victoria Ground, Stoke. There were no boys in our family but dad and I were close and often went on expeditions, so it was natural for him to include me in his football excursions. Sometimes we went on the train from our home in Meir, sometimes on the bus, and sometimes we cycled. There were always armies of little boys in the streets off Lonsdale Street, who would take our bikes into their back yards and guard them during the game, for a small consideration of course. It was 1944 and some Stoke players were returning from their army service, though I was too young to know the details.

Of course the star of the team was Stanley Matthews, and the chant of the supporters was, "Give it to Stan, give it to Stan". It was mesmerising to see him take off down the wing, leaving opposing defenders sprawling as he just bobbed past them with seeming ease. I read in his autobiography that he honed his skills as a youngster by dribbling a tennis ball along the pavement on the way to and from school. It was a dark day for Stoke when he was transferred to Blackpool. The manager at that time was Bob McGrory and he used to stand at the door of his office in his tweed jacket and homburg hat and glare. He never looked happy and the story I heard later was that his wife came down from Scotland with him, took one look at our fair city and caught the next train back North!

My best Christmas present was a ticket for the Butler Street stand on Boxing Day when Stan came back for the first time with his Blackpool team. Can't remember the result though.

Our usual match place was the Boothen End, behind the goal. I used to go in the boy turnstile and meet dad inside. The Stoke End was considered rough and there was no protection from rain and snow there. One match I remember it was snowing hard and the ground staff were brushing the lines continually. At half time Stoke were 2-0 down against Chelsea, but we beat the soft Southerners 3-2.

Stoke City's old Victoria stadium – painting by Gaz Williams, reproduced with permission of the artist

Later, I joined with school friends and went to neighbouring away games, like Manchester and Derby. We proudly wore our Stoke rosettes, though I have to admit that we hid them after the game rather than invite the hostile reactions.

Footballers in those days earned an average working class wage with a small bonus for winning - a pound per point – so they lived among us. No plush Cheshire mansions for them, they were council house lads who, like most youngsters, started their married lives with in-laws while they waited for their own council house or saved up for a deposit on a modest home, in Meir, Dresden, Stoke, Shelton, Norton. These were the days of the "£10 team"; almost all were local and had cost no more than their £10 signing on fee.

They travelled to and from the ground by bus, so with a little judicious time management we could travel on the same bus and, if brave enough, engage in conversation with them. It was all very friendly and innocent and for many years after I would see John Malkin, a winger, in the street, at an event, once at the swimming baths, and it was always, "Hello duck how are you?", he never knew my name! I got to know John McCue, a ferocious fullback, and a real gentleman. I would see him in church and later in the gathering of parents outside St Gregory's School when we collected our respective offspring.

My hero in those days was Neil Franklin, probably the best centre half of his day. He was always calm, cool and collected, rarely ended up on the ground, his shorts were always clean. His Stoke and England career came to an end when he was tempted to go to Bogota with the promise of better pay. Sadly, it didn't work out for him and he came back, but not to Stoke who refused to have anything to do with him and he went to Hull City. His wonderful career ended and he moved out of football into being a pub landlord, a job many ex-players seemed to do. I attended his funeral at St. Mark's in Shelton and the church was packed with Stokies, old school friends and with famous faces, Billy Wright, Nat Lofthouse, Stanley Matthews, Tom Finney and many more.

My personal sporting prowess was limited to hockey, which I loved because its rules, positions and aims were the nearest to football I could get. No women's football in those days. Dribbling down the wing I could feel like a Stan, defending I could be a Neil.

It all stopped once I left school as my job in the library service involved Saturday working, then when I met my future husband he was more interested in playing than watching. So my interest waned, but was awakened by the 1966 World Cup and now I am glued to Radio Stoke on Saturday afternoons, exchanging joyful or despairing texts with my oldest daughter who has inherited my dreams. At one point in her teenage years she did let down the side. She went out with a Port Vale supporter!

Last year I went to a reception at the Britannia Stadium and was delighted to see two great photos on the walls in Reception. One was, of course, Sir Stan and the other... yes it was my idol, Neil Franklin, and in one of the rooms was a wall devoted to his story. So the Potters forgave him and gave him the recognition he had earned.

Viv and her daughter Tina – both ardent Stoke supporters!

16. Ready: Racket Up

Joey Courchene

My name is Joey and I am 37 years old. I moved to Staffordshire in 2000 prior to attending university to study for a business degree. My passion for sport has been limited until somebody encouraged me to join the North Staffs Special Olympics. I have been an athlete with the Special Olympics for two years and I take part in athletics and badminton

It's been my love of badminton what I enjoy more however. I am in the North Staffs Special Olympics badminton team and I attend two-hour badminton sessions twice a week at Fenton Manor Sports Centre. Within the badminton group has two excellent volunteer coaches called Gemma and Derek. The rest of the team also commit themselves to the team by attending regularly and training hard for development of badminton as well as preparing for competitions. Gemma and Derek are proud of the team formed for not just the hard work we put in by regular attendance but also the success we have attained by the winning of medals at several events both at regional and national level.

Our badminton group has been several places such as Cardiff, Sheffield and Birmingham to take part in badminton competitions. Our endeavours are also merited by our commitments to fundraising money by organising fancy dress evenings, backpacking and sponsored walks. The monies raised enable us to compete in the events we have succeeded in

Badminton has made a difference to my life by helping me identify a sport I have a passion for as well as a sport I can develop. The North Staffs Special Olympics charity itself has also helped me to achieve this.

The Special Olympics is a renowned charity throughout the world that enables individuals with various disabilities to get involved in sport.

Stoke-on-Trent and North Staffordshire are fortunate to have a well-run and organised Special Olympics club to contain four sports offered to disabled athletes as sadly some parts of the United Kingdom do not have a Special Olympics club at all and if they did; they may only have one sport.

I feel the North Staffs Special Olympics charity has benefited the disabled community of North Staffordshire for sporting/cultural reasons and this is one reason why the City of Stoke-on-Trent has deserved the honour of being the European City of Sport for 2016.

17. Happy High Ropes

Kirsten Else

Kirsten wrote this entertaining story while a Year 6 pupil at Hillside Primary School, following a school trip to Stanley Head Outdoor Education Centre in Stoke-on-Trent.

On Wednesday 9th of June at 9:15, in Stanley Head's best classroom (it was the best because we were in it) thirty individuals sat on thirty tough, tight-filling chairs, waiting for their instructor's next move. Mr. Wilson shouted, "Groups B and C, you're with Mr. Rushton and me. Bring your sun-cream, your water bottles, and yourself. Meet us at the outdoor toilets in five minutes!" Ten minutes later, I found myself skipping down to the high rope course. For some, this would build confidence but for me it would be for fun.

At 9:30, I was geared up and practising for the five metre course. "Check" Maddie (my partner) shouted. After looking at her karabiners, I replied "Safe!" As we finished the course, Mr. Rushton gave us our helmets; they definitely weren't the height of fashion, but they were safe. While we were waiting for the others, I glanced round at the lofty, beige high rope behind me eagerly. I glanced at the field of elevated, saffron buttercups - which are poisonous - dancing in the breeze from the winds sigh.

When all of us had practised, we climbed over to the tower - the tower to the course. As Mr. Wilson clipped my cowtails to the wire, which was very thin, I looked out in the distance. In no time at all I had got to the punch bags. Calmed, relaxed, lulled, I went through the rest of the course. I realised - as I trekked down the stairs - I had climbed over the pearl-coloured nets; jumped over colossal gaps; dashed across the rope-bridges and balanced on the see-saws.

Once all of us did a bit, just four others went up to the ten metre course - me, Logan, Mr. Frost and Mr. Wilson. Once up there we went on a balancing log; a broken bridge and a sidewards rope trapeze. The worse part was when Mr. Wilson made me step right into a silver web, with a spider on it, a spider! One activity was a timber skateboard and you had to pull yourself across. I almost fell down twice on it; the last bit gave me the worst wedgie in the history of wedgies ever. At the end of it, I was sailing down off the parasailing machine.

As I trudged up to get my lunch, I thought about the activity. I remembered seeing Sam jumping on a log five metres of the ground and I had got higher than ever before - physically and emotionally. My advice to anyone doing high ropes (for the first time or not) is not to feel that you are going to fall five metres because you will be safe with your karabiners and cowtails - not to mention you are in a harness. I would love to do something like that again because I am a girl for heights. I know that if I ever do the high ropes again, I will think about my experience at Stanley Head OEC.

The High Ropes course at Stanley Head

18. Memories of My Father, Sir Stan

Jean Matthews Gough

Jean Gough is the daughter of Sir Stanley Matthews, and patron of the Sir Stanley Matthews Coaching Foundation. She has very generously shared this article (previously published on the Foundation's web site) and some photos from the family's photo albums as a very personal insight into Sir Stanley, the family man.

2016 is Stan's centenary year and as he has also been named as the Citizen of the 20th Century of Stoke-on-Trent, I thought it would be nice to share with you my memories of my father. As a little girl I remember him as a loving daddy who did his upmost to keep his family out of the limelight. In the 1940s Stan was the first sporting superstar and acclaimed all over the world. in spite of the fact that in those days there was no TV and little media. In order not to be recognised in the street he would go, as he thought, in disguise wearing sun glasses and a hat. It never worked.

Friday nights were always Film nights - especially cowboy films. As a family we always slipped on to the back row when it was dark and would slip out again before the playing of the national anthem for the King (George VI) and later the Queen (Elizabeth II).

I remember the discipline my Pop followed for himself but when I look back on this, he enjoyed his strict diet and his fitness regime. He often said he was keeping himself fit which he seriously wanted to do and he was getting paid for it!

I can see him now making his famous carrot juice every day. He managed to obtain a juicer that was tiny by today's standards. All visitors to the house were offered this magical health drink! The only trouble was that too much carrot juice could make your skin go yellow! However, he cut it down a little. I wish Stan were here today to use my today's juicer. He would love the blend of carrot, beetroot, celery, apple, broccoli, cucumber and tomato juice, my husband and I have every day. We notice that we don't have visitors around lunch time. I think they don't want us to inflict our juice on them!

Pop was obsessed by eating the right foods. He didn't insist that the family do this but we did become food conscious. I guess I passed this on to my own children. Stan's grand-daughter Samantha is a leading authority on nutrition in Texas and she and Pop used to have heathy eating discussions and they planned to write a book together, but sadly never got round to it. Stan loved steaks and salads. Everything used to have to be brown - bread sugar and even eggs!

A family picnic. From left: Stan, Stanley Junior, Betty and Jean

Stan's food ideals have rubbed off on me so I give my poor husband Bob a hard time with regards to his weight! Bob tells of an event that shows the humour and stirring character of Stan.

One day before a match at Stoke City we were enjoying the hospitality of the club. Stan whispers to Bob " Look Bob there's pork pies" Bob says "Thanks Stan!" and starts to eat one. Pop then calls across the room to me and says "Jean, Bob's got a pork pie".

As far as fitness is concerned I can see him now doing his deep breathing and stretching exercises before going for his workout on Blackpool's beach at 7am every day. Sometimes he would take me with him and I cherished this time with him. He would sprint a little, jog a little and walk a little to change pace, as it is done on the football field. His main aim was to be the fastest man in the world over 10 yards, so that he could skip around the defenders on the football pitch. One day whilst on the beach a fog came down and Pop lost his bearing and found himself walking into the sea. Somehow he managed to survive to tell us about it.

The day of any football game was the greatest day of all for Stan. It didn't have to be a Cup Match or Final - he cherished the atmosphere in the dressing room before every single match. He always had butterflies in his stomach and was sick just before a game so he ate nothing before the match. Then he would step on to the pitch and all nervousness was gone. Normally Stan was pretty even-tempered but the day before and the morning of a game the family kept very quiet! When playing for Blackpool and Stoke City Stan would walk to the ground with lead in his shoes so that when he put on his specially made lightweight football boots they felt like ballet shoes, so he could do his famous dash around the defence. Pretty clever if you think about it.

Stan was renowned for his sportsmanship and was never ever booked for a foul. That is not to say he didn't retaliate when he was at the mercy of some dirty play by a defender. He knew then that he then had the full back beaten, so he said nothing and retaliated with his feet by dribbling and passing. However, it has to be said that Pop was very competitive at home. Whatever game we were playing (even tiddlywinks) he had to win! I'm not saying he cheated but he was certainly not the same on the football field! If my brother and I were playing him at tennis and we had him a bit worried, he would say that he had to go and make an urgent phone call! Most of my family have inherited this competitive spirit so it makes for wonderful but rowdy get-togethers.

Stan was truly a real family man and I can remember the very happy years that we spent at our home The Grange in Blackpool. The house was always full of family and friends like Charlie Chester (Cheerful Charlie) the famous comedian of his day and his family. The home was full of warmth and laughter.

From the family album: Sir Stan with young Stanley

We had a secret signal which was our family sign, in which you placed the middle finger on the thumb to indicate we were a team Pop used to do this sign every time he ran out of the dressing room on to the pitch specially for us and only we saw it.

Pop was a very strict but warm and loving father. In my teenage years my social life was very limited and confined to the tennis club so it's not surprising that I met my husband Bob there. I was delighted to be allowed to go to the tennis club hop every month but even when I was nineteen Pop would be there at 10.00pm to take me home. Bob's earliest memory of me was when he looked round to have a dance with me and I'd gone already.

When I was nineteen I went round the world with the Blackpool football team. My mother and I were the only females in the party. We went to America, the Philippines, Australia and Hong Kong on a month long tour with the team, playing exhibition games. In Melbourne my brother Stanley Junior and I had tennis training with the legendary Harry Hopman. Can you imagine a teenager going round the world with a Premiership Football Team today! I often asked Pop before he died if he threatened trouble for any player who became friendly with me. Do you know I never got an answer to that question!

It amazes me that although it is now sixteen years since Stan died, he is still remembered not only for his football achievements, but as a warm and inspirational man. I very clearly remember going to Buckingham Palace in 1965 when he received his knighthood from the Queen. He was the first footballer to be knighted, whilst playing, which is still true today. The same year he played top flight football at the age of 50 - another record - and also became a grandfather when my son Matthew was born. Another first was being awarded the Football Writer's player of the year which incidentally he won twice - and he was the first recipient of the Ballon d'Or as the first European footballer of the year.

Since his death other awards continue to come. The Britannia Stadium statue which was erected by the Sir Stanley Matthews Foundation and shows the three phases of Stan's life as a Stoke City player, a Blackpool player and an England player. It is said to be the finest sporting statue in the country. Being a very modest man Stan was not moved by any of his triumphs but I think that being made the Citizen of the 20th Century of his home town Stoke-on-Trent would have meant a great deal to him because he loved all the people there and they loved him. Stan was a frequent visitor to his old school, Wellington Road, which is now St Luke's Primary School in Hanley. Can you believe his old classroom is still there along with other memorabilia. I think Stanley Matthews is on the curriculum!

People always liked to ask Pop if he wished he was playing today with the enormous wages of footballers. He would always answer "No, because I travelled the world for free and have friends all over". However, some things today have damaged the beautiful game. He would have been disgusted by the antics of some players on the field. He always travelled and had "itchy feet" and played in Malta, Canada, Australia, USA, Zimbabwe, Kenya, South Africa and South Korea - but he came back to his roots at Stoke for his last years.

In the 1950s he began his love of South Africa by going there as a guest player during the summer months, when there was no football at home. So, South Africa got into his blood and he returned every year to coach and play. In the 1970s he coached in the township of Soweto, which was considered to be dangerous during the apartheid years. He took the first team of black young players to leave South Africa for a tour to Brazil where they met Pele. The United Nations put Stan on the blacklist for entertaining in South Africa and banned him from the country. A bit ridiculous as he was coaching the black people! Stan said he was in good company as Frank Sinatra was also on the blacklist! However, Stan found his way in via Zimbabwe somehow. On his visit to Stoke-on-Trent in 2008 Bishop Desmond Tutu took Stan off the Blacklist and said he was so loved by South Africans that they called him "The Black Man with the White Face." Stan's love of Johannesburg spilled over to Bob and me as we went to live there for 14 years and where our three children grew up. Mandy our youngest was born there.

Even today South Africa is in my blood and I've been very privileged over several years to accompany 25 students from Stoke-on-Trent College to Cape Town where they coaching sport in the coloured primary and secondary schools. It brings a tear from me when a thousand pupils in one school alone remember Stan. It is wonderful for our family to know that he will still be remembered when we have gone. For this I'm so happy - and that there is a wonderful school named after him - Ormiston Sir Stanley Matthews Academy in Stoke-on-Trent. It is very apt that many of Stoke City Academy junior football players receive their education there.

The family today: Back – Samantha (granddaughter); Jean (daughter); Bob (son in law);
Front – Matthew (grandson); Stanley Jnr. (son); Mandy (granddaughter)

19. Aggression vs Fierce Fun: the Fine Line

Morwenna Hastings

Mowenna Hastings is a wheelchair basketball player, introduced to the game by her mother Tink, who helps coach the Stoke Spitfires team. Mo is an outstanding and passionate player who has just broken into the top level, representing Great Britain in an international competition earlier this year (2016).

"Fierce fun" "be fierce" phrases that have stuck in my head since my very first session with Tina Gordon (SDS and Basketball Scotland coach), and a skill that I have found quite challenging and to balance in my game.

Fierceness is a mindset, it's a state of mind that brings a psychological barrier up in your head, overpowering nerves and self-doubt to have a single tunnel vision on getting your 'focus face' on.

It's a state of mind that makes you never give up, it makes you want to achieve your best every time, pushing your limits and boundaries while still enjoying the game and having fun!

The difference between fierceness and aggression is that aggression makes you make mistakes, it means you take unsafe risks that result in fouls or make poor decisions that are unskilful due to having a sole focus that overtakes your mindset of rational thought and decision making.

I’ve seen aggressive players on court, genuinely they are in it purely for the win and usually from a selfish point of view that powers their aggressiveness to not play with their teammates but as a single man game creating weaknesses within their team.

I think that fierceness is taking pride in your game, using your teammates and being humble in both your strengths and weaknesses while not showing face to your opposition.

Being Scottish I have definitely been brought up with a strong sense of pride even when times are tough and hard, which I believe is where the Scots are renowned for this ‘never give up’ attitude, the strong characteristics of battling to the end regardless, which is where I can see how Scottish players in most sports are able to or should be educated in how to adjust into the 'fierce face' mask in our play.

When I play 'fierce' I want people to see me as a player not to be messed with, one that they will have to play 100% until the end because they know I'll never give up or give in, someone they can't take their eyes off because they are uneasy about what's going to happen next and someone that they can't mentally put off, as if coming across a brick wall.

Fierceness is about the mask you put on, unlike aggression where I believe the aggression is in the person and part of their characteristics I believe that fierceness is a mask that can be put on and taken off before and after games, where you as a player has to get into a mindset and get your head in the game through your own pre-game methods. Equally off court I think the fierceness is really shown because it gets taken away and you can be known for the person you are as an individual, showing your strength, focus and determination as a player.

I believe that fierceness is a forming of a barrier surrounding a player's head, holding in all the player's emotion and thoughts to give a blank mask of fierceness allowing accurate decision-making and skills to still be used through the mask of fierceness, whereas I think aggression is developed from the core of a player's head making it overpower decision-making and skill as the aggression will always come first and travel though any decisions the player makes, making the core of all decisions based on aggression as opposed to the player's decisions being made through the mask of fierce fun.

Fierceness is putting on a mask, a mask that never ever gives up, a mask that always gives 100% until the very end, a mask that cannot be read by other players, a mask that makes the player unpredictable and a mask that is always having focused fun on their ultimate goal.

On one wheel - Mowenna putting everything into defence representing Team West at the 2016 BWB Women's League All-Star Game; photo credit SA Images

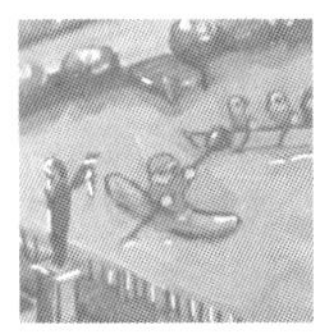

20. A White Water Ride – or a Life in Sport

Andrew Heaward

This is a great bit of writing about a journey through sport - and a serious love affair with kayaking. Great imagery too! Andrew has his own blog where he writes about all matters kayak.

I really didn't like sport at school, I was terrible at football, shocking at athletics and disinterested in just about every other sport. My sports journey started through Scouts; there I was introduced to a wide range of (to me) more exciting sports like grass skiing (which I hated), orienteering, climbing, hiking and an assortment of water sports. At the time only hiking really 'stuck' and for most of my youth you would find me trudging across Dartmoor with a big pack preparing for one long distance walking event or another.

My interests changed at university in Yorkshire where climbing and kayaking became part of my day to day life. I lived 15 minutes' walk from the Cow & Calf Rocks and about the same by car from the River Wharfe and the Student's Union had very active climbing and paddling clubs. Over my three years at university paddling quickly became my passion and I was out kayaking on white water somewhere at least twice a week almost without fail. I received some good coaching from club coaches, my skills rapidly improved, and because I was out so frequently so did my experience and critically, my confidence. Quickly I left grade two and three white water trips largely behind and with the support of a couple of equally ambitious friends started to really push myself, padding much harder and more risky grade four and five rivers, where the consequences of a mistake are often serious. At this time I was running complex rapids, fairly large waterfalls and thinking little of the potential consequences. I was in my twenties with no responsibilities and I was 'charging hard'.

Of course like any sporting career this wasn't always without incident. On one occasion a friend and I drove across to the Lake District through flooded roads and torrential rain, in one village on a hill we went through there was even three inches of water flowing downhill at a crossroads! This should have been a warning signal, but we were both young and fired up. We had set our sights on paddling the River Duddon a grade five test piece in the South Lakes that neither of us had done before. The guide book said, get in at a small bridge across the river with a section of flat water above. This was of course in the time before the advent of GPS so driving up the road we saw ahead of us exactly what seemed to be described in the guide book and preceded to make our normal shuttle arrangements, leaving cars at both the access and egress points for our trip down river. We however got it badly wrong and actually proceeded to launch onto Seathwaite Tarn Beck, a normally dry and vey rocky minor tributary of the Duddon, which due to the conditions had grown to look like a river itself and was running at a solid grade 5 on the day.

Once in, a small error about a hundred meters from our access point and I capsized with no chance to roll my kayak back up due to being knocked about by underwater rocks in the shallow but very rapid flow. This led to a long, rocky and at times fairly painful swim down about half a mile of what was now a raging torrent of white water with lots of drops and complex rapids. Eventually I managed to grab a tree branch and haul myself out onto the bank, standing up was however challenging as I had hit my right leg very hard on a rock whilst being thrown around in the water. Eventually I got up and leaning on my paddle went in search of my boat which had sped off downstream. I quickly found it, wedged mid flow in a four foot waterfall, full of water and firmly pinned vertically.

A kayak full of water can easily weigh a ton so as you can imagine for two of us extracting this was quite a task. Once it was freed I found the nose of my lovely blue plastic Pyranha Magic Bat kayak had been bent up at a forty-five-degree angle and was completely beyond repair, signalling the end of this trip and time for a new boat! Driving home was a real challenge, as was walking for about ten days afterwards but like most sports injuries it was my pride that was hurt most! After a short while I was back on the water pushing my limits once again, although this time in a shiny new kayak, thank heavens for student loans!

It's funny how injuries don't put you off, and how you can rationalise potentially life threatening incidents and still continue. I was soon back on the water, within a year not only I had completed some coaching awards, but I was also chairman of the college canoe club. It wasn't just personal progression that was driving me at this time but also a strong drive to get others involved and see them experience the fun I get from the sport.

Graduation from university brought huge changes for my paddling: I returned home to Devon, joined a local club and due to the nature of the club dialled back the kinds of white

water I was paddling a little. For several years I climbed and surf kayaked in the summer, then ran rivers when it rained in the winter. This period saw me take my first paddling trip abroad, two weeks in the glorious French Alps exploring amazing white water rivers around the hilltop town of Briancon including white water classics like the Chateau Queyras Gorge on the River Guil, and the Durance Gorge.

At that time I also worked for Devon County Council's Youth Services, and led a project helping young people from rural villages plan and deliver their own outdoor activity programmes. As with many people however my career took a few twists and turns, and quickly work became my main focus and my paddling suffered. I moved to the Midlands for work, joined a new canoe club and for a while was active as both a paddler and coach, whilst this wasn't the most active period of my paddling career, I did manage my second foreign trip and spent two weeks exploring the exciting high volume rivers of Austria and Switzerland including one incredible trip down the River Vorderrhein in Switzerland that involved traveling to our access point fully kitted up with our kayaks aboard the local train service! Sadly once again work intervened and for almost ten years I didn't paddle, although the desire to never left me.

About four years ago I came to an important personal decision, work matters, but so do the other things in life I love. I returned to paddling, updated my coach qualifications, took my formal river leadership qualification and got involved in a local club.

This process let me to attend a White Water Safety and Rescue course on the river Tees, the irony of which will soon become apparent. The first day of the course was a lot of fun, involving swimming in rapids and exploring rope systems to rescue people and equipment from the river. At the end of the day, I entered the river to act as dummy casualty for some simple kayak-to-swimmer rescues. Unfortunately I was tired and giving it no real thought, so I jumped in, moving maybe one metre forward with no vertical fall. Wow what a mistake! As soon as I hit the water I knew things had gone badly wrong, my right foot had hit a submerged rock and I was now floating in the water and could feel my foot moving completely separately from the rest of my leg. The poor paddler who came to rescue me expecting a 'mocked up' incident got the shock of his lifetime: instead I had to persuade him I had actually really hurt myself. He helped me get to the side and I dragged myself up onto a shingle beach leaving my injured leg in the cold water cradled by my other foot. Help soon came and the emergency services were called, unfortunately I was about a mile from the road and at the bottom of a steep rocky slope.

Once the paramedics arrived I was able with the help of some pain relief and an amazing inflatable splint to climb with help to the top of the bank and was then stretchered to a nearby field where the Cumbria Air Ambulance had landed to bring a doctor to check out my injury. After a little debate about cutting me out of my expensive dry suit, which I wasn't having any of, I was helped out of this and the doctor was able to diagnose that I had badly broken both bones in my right leg, however otherwise I was ok - so they sent me to hospital by ambulance instead of getting a ride in the helicopter! In fact I had managed to break my leg in three separate places and ended up with several pins and was off work for about five months whilst I healed. This didn't stop me paddling once I was fit again.

I'm over forty now and I will never again be the 'charging hard' paddler I was in my twenties, now I have too many other responsibilities, less flexibility and perhaps more sense. But my passion for kayaking remains just as strong. Today I coach on a regular basis and lead trips for my club, the Potteries Paddlers, both to introduce novices to the delights of white water kayaking on easier water and help our more experienced paddlers to enjoy the UK's many more challenging grade three to four white water rivers. I'm also an active part of the club in many other ways and I do whatever I can to help it grow and prosper so others can benefit from the exciting, challenging and formative experiences that my sport has given to me.

In the world of kayaking I was once lucky enough to meet an inspirational Staffordshire man by the name of Donald Bean who I met on the water at an event on the North Tyne river. Sadly, Donald is no longer with us, but he paddled challenging white water well into his eighties, including many notable expeditions even after he retired. Donald wasn't an 'excellent paddler' but he left a legacy in the sport that few can claim, not one of first descents or extreme kayaking, but one filled with adventure, passion and a respect for others. He did so much to inspire and enthuse others to get involved in this amazing sport, I'd like to think that one day in the distant future I can look back at my time and have achieved just a little of what Donald did.

This is what a life in sport means to me.

21. My Dancing Poem

Meg Higgins

This is a lovely poem about dance, from Meg Higgins. Meg wrote this at a Middleport community event (see page 45) - and illustrated it beautifully too!

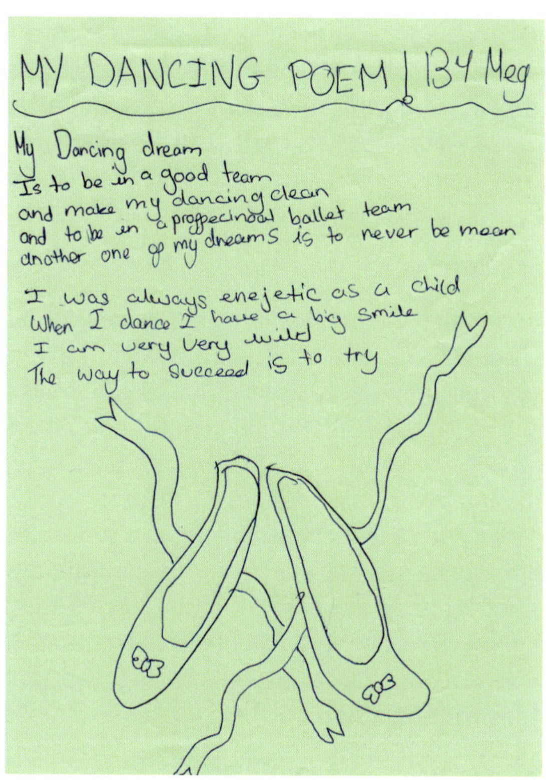

22. The Stoke-on-Trent City of Sport UK Triathlon

Peter Hooper

Dawn breaks on the 25th September. It's time to get the dogs out for their run along the towpath, and for me to run through my mental checklist of everything I need for my first triathlon later in the day. There's so much to think of: swimming gear, cycling gear and running gear; mandatory gear; optional gear; new gear; old gear. No wonder triathlon gear is an industry in its own right – for the dedicated, it's not just swimming gear, it's triathlon swimming gear (check); it's not just cycling gear, it's aerodynamic helmet (nope), carbon-framed bike (nope), aerobars to get as low as possible on the bike (nope). At least the running gear is mostly just running gear, unless there's a page in the catalogue I've missed somewhere.

That said, my big concession to the tri is my tri-suit, which I'll wear throughout – the swim, bike and run stages. "Is that new?" my wife asks suspiciously as I parade around in all-in-one lycra – she seems completely immune to the charms of a slightly overweight middle-aged man posing around in sports gear designed for athletes half his age.

It's still dark on the towpath and there's six hours to go still until my 12.15 start time, but part of the reason for the early start is making sure I get a proper breakfast down me before heading to Trentham for the start of the Elite races at around 8.30. It's partly the chance to see how things like transition are done, partly just to see some outstanding athletes at the top of their game. The event is being held at Trentham Lake, about half an hour drive's away. Once I've had breakfast, double-checked I've got all the gear, and struggled into the tri-suit then it's time to go.

It's going to be a busy morning spectating: there's a 'Fun' tri event to kick things off; then the Super Sprint (374m swim, 10km bike and 2.5k run); then the Elite Women, followed by the Elite Men, both doing the Olympic distance (1500m swim, 40km bike and 10k run); then the Olympic distance for 'ordinary' men and women, predominantly club members; and finally the Sprint event, which I'm registered for – first up the Sprint Men, then the combined hordes of the Sprint Women and the Sprint Relay teams – the Sprint distance being a 750m swim, a 20km bike and a 5k run. The swim course that we all tackle is a 375m circuit marked out by buoys in the lake (so two laps for the Sprint distance), followed by a 600m run from the lake back to the main transition area, necessitating a 'Shoe Transition' to allow swimmers to exit the lake and put on running shoes before racing back to the bikes.

When I get to Trentham it's a hive of activity. Registration has been open since 6.30, and the car park is starting to fill up with vehicles laden with expensive-looking tri gear. I chat to some of the City of Sport team who are helping on the day and am heartened to meet a couple of Sprint Male competitors, novices like me. I register and get a bag of goodies, including labels to go on every conceivable surface of the bike – handlebars, seat tube, front of helmet, side of helmet – plus tattoo transfers of my number (510) to go on my arm and calf. And a swim hat, race numbers, safety pins, energy gels and more…

I make my way down to the pontoon where the races start, in time to catch the Fun and Super Sprint swimmers. I start to wonder if I've been a bit ambitious entering the Sprint category. Maybe a shorter swim would have been a good idea: it's not my strong suit. Then it's the elite swimmers' turn – elite women first. Wetsuits are compulsory for the Olympic distance because of the time they're in the water. They're optional in the Sprint event but with the water temperature a measly 16 degrees I'm not sure my plan to swim in just the tri suit is the best one – on the other hand, I've entered a Chill Swim event in the Lake District in December where wetsuits aren't allowed, so part of the mission today is acclimatisation to colder water…

I watch the Elite race start, then it's time to grab a coffee and start getting my gear organised. Sticking stickers, applying transfers, pinning on numbers, finding a space in the transition area to rack my bike, catch up with a few friends and former work colleagues in the crowd and trying to calm last minute nerves. I'm used to big race atmospheres at marathons and cycle sportives, but this is new territory for me: not just the three disciplines but the unknowns as well – I've only done one mass-start swim event, I've never done transitions, I've no idea if I'll physically be able to ride a bike after what is a big swim for me – or be able to run on the back of the cycle ride. There's endless potential for very public humiliation given the size of the crowds and the presence of TV cameras, which makes me even more nervous.

All too quickly it's time to strip to the tri suit, put on my 'run transition' shoes and head for the pontoon, feeling seriously under-dressed amongst the spectators heading in the same direction. On the pontoon, once we've been called forward, I look in vain for any other triathletes *not* in a wetsuit. As far as I can tell, I'm the only one braving the water without one. This is worrying. I'm distracted by a tap on the shoulder from the guy behind me. "You know you can leave your trainers in the shoe transition area…" – I glance down and realise I'm still clad in running shoes! Whoops. Back to T1 to shed my shoes and line them up with all the other pairs, and then back on the pontoon. I had expected a mass run and dive into the water, a la Hawaii Ironman, but instead we're asked to swim out to a notional start line between buoys at the start of the course, where around a hundred of us bob around in the surprisingly cold water until the starter judges that the field is ready – and we're off!

I've played this bit of the triathlon out in my head in the wee small hours of most nights of the previous week, along the lines of: … *I hang back at the start so as not to get swamped by faster swimmers; the faster swimmers (there's about ninety-nine of them) lap me anyway when I'm about halfway around the first circuit; I'm pretty much on my own for the start of the second circuit, but not for long because the Sprint Women's and Sprint relay team's start time is only 15 minutes after the Sprint Male start - by the time I'm rounding the top buoy and half way round my second circuit the entire women and relay wave of swimmers will be bearing down on me; I stagger out of the water at the same time as the fastest Sprint women competitors...*

And this is exactly as it plays out. The first lap goes slowly and steadily, no need to panic that I'm behind everyone else, that's where I expect to be. I find a brief spurt of energy at the start of the second circuit, hoping to round the top buoy before I get caught up in the next wave – but in trying to go faster I ship an appreciable amount of Trentham Lake, which is by now a black soup of mud and weed. And then my left calf cramps up. This wasn't in my plan. I can only kick with one leg. My coughing and spluttering and general impression of a non-swimmer attracts the attention of one of the kayakers who are providing safety cover. "All right?" she asks, as she paddles over. "Yes, just wish I learned how to swim better..." I reply. My breaststroke has descended to something more akin to doggy paddle by now, and half way down the final leg, with the pontoon still looking forever away, my right calf starts cramping off and on, alternating with my left one.

My personal rescue kayaker – she's clearly decided I'm on the verge of drowning so is shadowing my every effort – is quite keen for me to grab the nose of her boat and either have a rest or get towed in. "I'm fine" I splutter. I think we both know I'm lying through my teeth but obstinate male pride makes me battle on. I don't want to give up with the pontoon now frustratingly close, so painfully slowly and with the fastest women swimmers now finishing ahead of me, I struggle on and finally, finally reach the pontoon where I get hauled out by a friendly marshal. I'm sure I hear a sigh of relief from my guardian angel kayaker. Thank you, kayaker lady, whoever you are, for being there – I'd have been in trouble without your reassuring presence.

Image courtesy New Pixels Events Photography

I stagger down the pontoon feeling completely shot and chilled to the bone. The agony of my cramped calves seems to have gone but that might just be because I've lost all feeling in my extremities. Amazingly, I manage a jog/limp to the shoe transition area and struggle into my running shoes - a spare pair so that my race shoes are dry for the 5k – and set off at an unsteady run for the bike transition.

A 'proper' triathlete will be in and out of transition in a matter of a minute or two, but I'm there drying off, trying to get my running shoes off, trying to get my cycling shoes on and generally being hopeless for over ten minutes, shivering violently. The next big worry - I'm a bit of a worrier - that had played through my mind in those earlier sleepless nights was of being unable to change gears on the bike because my fingers were too numb.

But actually the bigger issue is my shivering. For the whole of the first lap of the cycle route – up and down the A34 dual carriageway from Monkey World to Stone and back – it's all I can do to keep a straight line and not impede the other cyclists on the route. There are cyclists everywhere – mostly overtaking me, although it's a great feeling to catch and overtake a few myself. At this stage in the triathlon I'm in a completely random mix of Olympic distance male and female triathletes, slower Sprint males on their final lap, and the whole of the Sprint female and Sprint relay cyclists.

The second 10km lap on the bike is better now that I'm warming up a bit, helped by the sun coming out – it's amazing the difference in temperature between the shaded sections of road and the sunny sections. Back in transition, I dismount (with difficulty) on the dismount line, walking the bike back to the rack (running being beyond me), before taking my helmet off, swapping cycle shoes for running shoes for the final leg, and setting off for the run.

Image courtesy of New Pixels Events Photography

The start of the 5k run route passes near the finish zone and the (impressive) massed ranks of spectators, so I suck my stomach in and make the best pretence of running that I can for the first kilometre or so, until a slight uphill gradient (1:100) reawakens my twitchy calves – they were grumpy throughout the bike section, but are now threatening serious industrial action. Some twinges can be ignored and run through, but this is in the "stop or I'll go twang" category, so the rest of the run section passes in an alternating walk:shuffle eternity. Even so, I manage to catch a few other runners who have similarly ground to a walk, and even attempt to give an impression of a sprint as the finish line approaches.

Image courtesy of New Pixels Events Photography

I grind to a halt as soon as I'm through the finish arch and desperately want to throw up until I remember C4 are filming the event - I really don't want to go viral on YouTube. I hold myself together, collect my finishers medal and swear "Never, ever, again". Ticked that box, done a triathlon, can call myself a triathlete, on to the next challenge.

Two days later I get the results and my splits. Two hours six minutes for the tri Sprint distance. Hmmm. The swim was slow, slow, slow, I think to myself– surely I could shave minutes off the time split there if I learnt how to swim properly and wore a wetsuit? And that T2 time of ten minutes – criminal. And if I hadn't got so cold and had cramp, then there's time to be had on the bike. And a bit more training and more of the 5k would be runnable, surely? Sub-two hours has got to be do-able. When's the next one?!

Thanks to Stoke-on-Trent European City of Sport, the Trentham Estate and Triathlon UK – it was a blast! What a great event. I would recommend it to anyone. My only advice would be to train. And wear a wetsuit. And learn to do front crawl...

STOKE-ON-TRENT
UKTriathlon
Because life is better
when you
'tri'

23. The Love of My Life

Ron Hughes

This entertaining short story was recounted by Ron to his daughter Jan Garner. Ron has dementia, but still has wonderful memories of growing up in Hanley and of his life-long love affair with Stoke City. It's a great read alongside Viv Cotton's story on p.84, with her memories of the same era.

We lived in Ward Street in Northwood (Hanley) and played where Northwood Stadium now is. We played every Sunday and met on Margaret Street at Barker's Pub and travelled all over the place including the area along Leek Road called 'The Steps' and Hanley Park. We called ourselves 'The Ward Street Wanderers'.

As kids, all the boys loved football and we often walked from Northwood to Shelton, Leek Road or wherever else there were a group of like-minded lads.

We all supported both Stoke City and Port Vale, going to all the games. To watch the Vale we used to go through the Church yard, move a piece of tin and get in through the men's toilets.

When we went to Stoke's Victoria Ground we always walked through Hanley Park. I loved watching Denis Herrod and Neil Franklin who was a great centre half and who never had to be spoken to by the ref for fouling! He went abroad for more money, but it didn't work out. I also remember that the right back was a school teacher called John McCue. In those days the players usually ended up covered in mud and sometimes you could not tell who was who!

Memories of the Victoria

Pride of Boslem 1

Reproduced with permission of the artist, Paine Proffitt

I delivered coal in a wheelbarrow every Saturday morning to earn the money to get into the Boothen End with my brother and our mates.

Once I reached 14 I worked in the Pots and we often played football and cricket at lunchtime, and we played against other departments and firms after work.

In the 60s and 70s, we usually went to Rhyl in the Potter's Fortnight*, where we stayed at Sunny Vale Holiday Camp (an old army barracks). Most evenings before tea lots of us dads and the kids would set up a footie game with jumpers for goal posts. We still all played in our day clothes and shoes – I've never had a pair of trainers or football boots but I had a pair of pumps in the 1950s when I went on holiday to the Isle of Man.

I've always loved football and I'm still a season ticket holder for Stoke and also love to listen to matches on the Radio or watch them on the TV.

** Potters Fortnight – the last week of June and the first week of July was a two-week holiday when all the Stoke-on-Trent factories shut down and the City emptied.*

24. My Sporting Story: Athletics

Emma Jackson

Emma Jackson is one of Stoke-on-Trent's outstanding athletes, who has represented England at 800m in every age group. She was the fastest junior in the world in 2007 and in that year also won a silver medal at the European Junior Championships. In 2011 she reached the semi-finals of the World Championships and after a spell out with injury has recently represented England again at an international meet.

When I was five years old I said that I when I grew up I wanted to be an author or a runner. At that age I don't think I'd ever done any running or writing but I obviously had some childish intuition of where my talents lay. My writing career is yet to take off but running has been my life for nearly 20 years. It is in my blood - my mum and dad even met at an athletics track. (The story goes that my dad was so besotted with my mum on their first meeting that he walked her all the way home only to realise that he'd cycled to the track and had to go all the way back for his bike.)

Funnily enough though, my first foray into racing was nothing to do with my parents. A girl in the year above me at St. Joseph's College, Kate Sherratt, saw that I was pretty competitive at sports day and invited me along to a race that she was doing in Manchester. The race was a cross-country course which involved periodically jumping over hay bales. I was only nine years old and had never done anything like it before. My dad came with me and just told me to "stay as close to Kate as possible"... I took his advice rather literally. I followed Kate from gun to tape, she finished 16th and I finished 17th. It never occurred to me to go past her.

I loved my first outing and promptly joined Newcastle Staffs AC. My first coach was Arthur Shaw, a wonderful man who must have been in his 70s when he coached me yet was still known to do handstands at the side of the track. Training was mainly about having fun. Of course some parts were tough (hill reps up Keele Bank certainly stand out in my memory) but the emphasis was on enjoyment and building a well-rounded individual. We were always encouraged to try other events, with varying success rates. I could do a decent long-jump but my first attempt at doing the 'Fosbury Flop' high-jump resulted in me kneeing myself in the face and a broken nose (my mum and dad choosing not to take me to the hospital as there was 'nothing they could do' and instead went to get fish and chips for tea and left me in the car with my face pouring with blood). I decided to stick to running after that.

Arthur's group was very successful and our team won many regional and national titles. All of the girls were great friends on and off the track. However, when the Stoke-on-Trent school cross-country races came around we were no longer a team and became bitter rivals. The top girl in our group was called Leanne Finney. I had never beaten her in a race but was just as good in training. Before the cross-country race hosted by St. Joseph's College, my home fixture, my dad told me that he thought that I could win today. I panicked, started crying and told my dad off for putting pressure on me. I learnt a valuable lesson that day... Always listen to your dad, I won.

I loved those Stoke Schools Cross-Country races. Everyone at school knew me as 'the runner' and I loved showing them what I could do. One race at Holden Lane School was a bit of a complicated course so they asked an older boy to be a hare and run in front of us all to show us the way. However, after about 200m I decided that he was too slow and was getting in the way so I strode past him. I'm told he pulled out soon after looking rather sheepish.

Unfortunately, Arthur retired from coaching when I was 12 years old. There were no other coaches at Newcastle AC so my dad took over for a while. He was probably hoping for a Peter and Seb Coe type dynamic but it ended up more like Homer and Bart Simpson. I have the utmost respect for anyone in authority and I had always unquestioningly done whatever training Arthur had told me to do but for some reason I did not extend the same respect to my dad. I moaned, I argued and I refused to do any session he set me. It wasn't long before he sent me off to Stoke AC.

I certainly never argued with the training that Alan Morris set me at Stoke. I was the youngest in the group by quite a way and some of the girls were my heroes. Emma Ward was the only person ever to win every single English Schools title at every age-group. The English Schools is the equivalent of the Olympics to a school child and she had won it SIX times. I don't think I dared to speak for the first few weeks. The group took me under their wing though and I was soon christened 'Little Em'.

This was proper training now. Battling against the elements at Northwood Stadium is not for the faint-hearted. Built on the side of a hill, it is known by all athletes nationwide as 'the windy track'. I am convinced that it is always a good two degrees colder at Northwood than anywhere else. The sessions were tough and I was trying to keep up with girls a lot older and better than me. Despite this, I still have such happy memories of those days. I progressed rapidly by training with such a good group and there were some real characters in the group so there was always a laugh to be had.

When it came to leaving school and all my friends were choosing universities, I knew that there was only one choice for me, it had to be Keele. I had many people telling me to go to Loughborough as it was THE university for runners but there was no way I was going to leave Alan and Stoke AC. I had progressed so well over the years. Aged 19 I was easily the number one 800m runner in the country and I had run the fastest time in the world for an under 20. I had no intention of leaving my coach, my family, my support network and my home-town.

In the same way that I loved being 'Little Em' at training (despite being easily the tallest in the group by now), I have never been more proud than when I was known as 'Our Emma' in the local media when I ran in the 2010 Commonwealth Games and I was astounded by the public outcry in Stoke when I was overlooked for the 2012 Olympics. It got me through a very tough time knowing that so many people were on my side. Despite being injured for a couple of years now, the number of people I run past who shout me on and wish me well is incredible. I don't think I ever pass another runner who doesn't bid me good day.

The kindness of strangers in this city never fails to amaze me. While I want to achieve great things for myself, I truly want to achieve them for the people of Stoke-on-Trent as well. I want to show the world just what us Stokies can do.

25. Carrying a Torch: The Arrival of the Olympic Flame in Staffordshire

Glenn James

To celebrate TeamGB's success in the 2016 Rio Olympics, we thought it would be good to rewind the clock to 2012 and the local start of the London Games, as the Olympic flame travelled through Staffordshire. Local author Glenn James sent us a wonderful bit of writing he did at the time, capturing everything that is great about the Olympics.

Glenn and his wife Angela run Unleash, a new arts organisation committed to encouraging and promoting literacy and the literary arts.

A fire is spreading its way around the British Isles. It has captured the imagination of the people everywhere and it is spreading a kind of fever, both before it and in its wake. Where ever it goes, alongside the athletics enthusiasts, people who have previously had little or no interest in sport are turning out into the streets in their thousands, to welcome it, and cheer it on its way. Carried in ancient tradition by a torch bearer, held proudly head high, it forges its way through the crowds and bursts forth into huge gold cauldrons... To sleep in little Davey Lamps, before going on its way again, leaving unforgettable memories behind it.

It hasn't even reached London yet, but the Olympic Flame of 2012 has well and truly set Britain ablaze. Thousands will cherish special memories of this unique, once in a lifetime progress, and writer Glenn James and his family saw it arrive in Staffordshire...

At the BBC, the tickets to see the Olympic Flame lit in Stoke-On-Trent were gone, almost before the radio presenter had finished announcing they were available. The arrival of the flame in the Potteries was so madly anticipated that they went like lightening. But I had a mission. The Olympic Flame would be arriving on my daughter Elizabeth's third birthday, and seeing it lit was one present I was really determined she was going to have. So I kept my ear to the ground and as soon as I heard that tickets were available again, I was off the starting blocks faster than a Gold Medallist. I'm proud to say my vigilance paid off and I proudly returned home with tickets for the big night!

The Torch would be making its way through Cheshire during the day, to arrive for its evening rest in Hanley, Stoke-On-Trent, at about 7.30pm in the evening on the 30th of May. We were ready in good time, and my wife Angela and I, Elizabeth herself, and her older sister Charlotte set off early. I have never known an atmosphere like it on that journey, there was really something in the air, a kind of fizzing excitement. I'm not particularly superstitious, but a week before I had shaken hands with a chimney sweep, who cheerfully slapped me on the shoulder and said "Good luck is with you now, mate, you wait and see!" Well it certainly was that evening, as it was one which proved to be an incredible night to remember.

We were worried that we had taken longer than we anticipated getting into town and we really hurried along the last few streets. The Torch was due to arrive in Hanley Park and as we got closer we passed fleets of Police vans, whose officers cheerfully pointed us in the right direction. We were in no doubt about our destination, as when we sighted the streets surrounding the Park itself, they were thickly lined with people out to see the torch bearer arrive with the Olympic flame. They were also going bananas and we ran now, convinced that we were going to miss it.

I would have laughed if he had recounted such a thing a week before, but you know, this is where my friend the chimney sweep's luck began to kick in. We ran down to join the crowd, the two of us with a three year old and an eight year old, and on arriving we went to lift the children up so that they could see over the throng. The crowd was about six people deep where we joined it, but on seeing that we had two small children, they parted like the red sea to let us in to the front! Wonderful, I can't think of anywhere I have been where people have been so thoughtful. And how incredible that they did exactly that just at that point... we hardly had time to catch our breath, when the golden coach which carries the flame and the torch bearers, drew up right in front of us, as if it were a bus stopping to let us on! I cannot convey our sheer disbelief of how this happened, exactly in front of us, JUST as we GOT to the front, it was just dumbfounding.

We were about two metres from the door, and as we looked on in disbelief, the Torch Bearer got out smack in front of us, and set foot on Staffordshire soil with the Torch, right before our astounded eyes.

This was 25 year old Ainsley Cooper, a brave and valiant athlete, who suffers severely from autism, epilepsy, and learning difficulties. He stepped down with great grace and dignity and as he began to make his way with the torch, the crowd just went absolutely berserk. Accompanied by his father, Will, he made his way gently along the approach to the park, as cheerleaders in blue danced ahead of him heralding the flame and the huge gold coach made its stately way behind them both.

Of course, we wanted to get into the park too to see the flame lit, so we set off at a run ourselves along the backs of the crowd lining the road. This is the part I cannot forget, dashing madly along behind that huge well behaved crowd with everyone in Holiday mode, and looking back over my shoulder to see the cheerleaders advancing in our wake. The roar of the crowd followed us all along the road like a wave of joy, and the atmosphere was unforgettable. I have seen huge civic functions, rock concerts, and massive New Year's Eve parties, but this was something really special.

Luckily, we made it into the park itself with time to spare, as the flame was due to change bearers on its way to the cauldron, and we joined the massive crowd around the stage. It was a wonderfully cheerful crowd, filled with a tangible anticipation you could almost taste, and we made our way forward through it with little difficulty. Charlotte, our elder daughter, wanted to get close to the area where the runner would come in, so I made my way in that direction with her and lifted her up in my arms. No sooner did I do that than she flung out an arm and pointed, with a cry of "Look!! Look Daddy, there it is!!"

Carried by Imran Sherwani, (Stoke's previous Gold Medallist of 1988), and about 20 feet in front of us, we saw the golden torch held aloft over the heads of the crowd and advancing towards the stage at speed in the hand of its bearer. The place just *erupted.* People were shouting and screaming, punching the air with joy, and jumping up and down, so it was very hard to get a photograph... mainly because I was shouting and screaming, punching the air, and jumping up and down myself! I got a great close-up photo of the back of someone's head when I tried to get a picture of the flame touching the cauldron. When they actually lit the cauldron the roar of the crowd would not have disgraced an Iron Maiden Concert and it took quite a while for my ears to recover! "Stoke-on-Trent, this is your time to SHINE!!" the presenter shouted as the cauldron was lit, and if there had been a roof in the locality it would have been well and truly raised by the cheering.

We were then treated to a full on Greacian ballet in mid air, as performers from the New Vic Theatre put on an amazing display above our heads, suspended from a giant crane and performing on long silk ribbons around an open bell framework. This phenomenal display certainly did credit to Staffordshire in some style, as performers in ancient Greek Dress simultaneously performed on the stage around the flame itself, burning brightly in its caludron.

This pretty much blew everyone away. It was an amazing finale and after seeing the Flame consigned safely to its little Davey Lamp for the night, we thought that was very much the end of the evening. People steadily had their pictures taken before the Olympic Cauldron, then happily went on their way to see what the concession stands had to offer. Feeling really hyped up by the experience, and gloriously happy, we were no exception... but there was one last great treat left in store for the evening...

We shortly afterwards discovered that there was an opportunity to have your photograph taken by the official Coca-Cola sponsers, holding the Olympic Torch. It goes without saying that it's a great British tradition to queue for things, but we didn't mind this a jot! We were able to stand together as a family and hold that famous beacon which would soon be heading, by a circuitous route, for the stadium in London, having been collected from Athens itself by Princess Anne. It was an incredible feeling, a defining moment for us as a family, and an fantastic momento for our daughters' birthday. I will shake hands with a chimney sweep again when I see one, and if it's the same guy, I'll buy him a pint!

We were not particularly interested in athletics, but this great ceremonial procession bought everyone together as a community. Stoke-on-Trent certainly showed it can put on a stunning event and we went away just a little bit more proud of where we live. Perhaps that's what it's all about really, instilling that unity as a community. Everyone there will have shared in that feeling, that pride and joy and exhilaration, and will take away undying memories of what the evening was like, even photographs like us, of having held that famous torch for a moment in their hands.

That experience is spreading, a unifying pride at a time when we could all do with something uplifting, to pull us together as communities and put a bit of spring back in our heels. The torch continues its progress and all I can say in conclusion, when I consider how many people held it before us and how many would be doing so in future is "There are eight million stories in the naked city. This has been one of them."

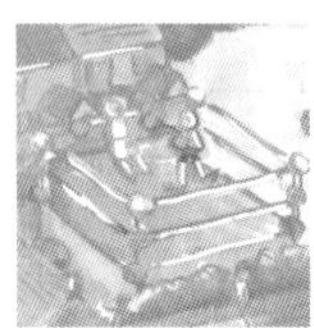

26. A Few Memories of Klondike Bill

Barbara Jones

We met Barbara Jones at a community lunch in Bentilee, and were delighted when she let us have this evocative article on wrestling greats from the 1960s and 70s. This piece was previously published in the Bentilee Magazine and is reproduced here with Barbara's permission.

A few years ago I was fortunate enough to meet and become friends with some well-known wrestlers from around the country. I met many of them while they were working for Orig Williams from a base in Rhyl. Amongst my favourites were Mighty Chang, Klondike Kate (who lives in Bentilee even as I type), Frank Cullen, Steve Peacock and Johnny Palance. My most favourite of all though was Klondike Bill who sadly is no longer with us. He was the twenty-nine stone hero who fought people like Giant Haystacks and Big Daddy, and sometimes tagged with Klondike Jake, his ring partner.

While living at the house owned by Orig, Klondike also ran the house, which was let as holiday flats. When the season ended we stayed on, and moved to the top floor, which we shared with Steve Peacock, Rusty Blair, and Gloria who was the Cherokee Princess. We became close friends with Klon, and I remember him as being a warm, friendly, loveable man, with a heart as big as himself. My husband and he worked together up and down the country, on the holiday camps, in the summer. Sometimes I went along to watch and sell programmes. I remember one night in Liverpool Stadium, when the fans tried to turn Klondike's car over, with us in it! A very hair-raising experience, I can tell you. It didn't bother Klon though, it was all part of life's rich tapestry to him. He made a joke of it whilst we panicked.

Most evenings after working we would all end up in the Morville Hotel in Rhyl. It was right next door to where we lived. And sometimes we would go on to a nightclub in the town. We had good times and long happy summers. Most spare time was spent in Klondike's basement flat. We made wine, grew tomatoes in growbags, while Klon had a fad on being self-sufficient turning the basement yard into an allotment, drinking tea and chatting, putting the world to rights. There was always someone dropping in, and they were all made welcome. We spent hours listening to Klondike's tales of working abroad in Hong Kong and Dubai. His stories were fascinating and he never had any shortage of listeners. Being a Yorkshire man, he could rattle on forever.

Christmas came round and Klondike decorated the hall with streamers and a huge tree. Some of us came in a bit the worse for drink after a good night on the town, and decided to have a party on the top floor. It got a little high-spirited and someone decided to hide the tree while playing the 1812 overture at full bore, at five o'clock in the morning! Klondike discovered his tree was missing and his sultry tones - MORE LIKE VESUVIAS WAS ERUPTING - could be heard at Splash Point, demanding to know who was responsible. He saw the funny side, as he always would, and ended up laughing - although he'd gotten little or no sleep with all the noise. I rarely saw him in a bad mood - if he was, everybody got out of his way!!

To watch him in the ring was pure magic. He had a great following on the circuit, and was loved by all, young and old alike. The kids doted on him, and he was never too busy to sign autographs, no matter how tired he was. Towards the end of his career, even though he was quite ill, he never let the punters down, and would insist on getting in the ring no matter what. To him the public came first - and he was a showman to the end. When he was advised to give up wrestling, he ignored all warnings, saying it was only life he knew, and the only one he wanted.

Klondike Bill – image courtesy of Wrestling Heritage

Such was the case when he was working in Scotland. Sadly, he collapsed and died in the dressing room after thrilling his audience to the last.

To me he will always be one of the best friends I ever had, and my life became the richer for him being a chunk of it.

As long as wrestling goes on, he will be remembered as part of this wonderful sport. The few years I spent around the professional wrestlers that this article is dedicated to are well remembered, with more than a fondness and a small tinge of sadness, but most of all with a big Thank You to them for all their contribution to a wonderful sport, and for being the showmen and women that keep the punters coming back for more. An extra thanks goes to our own Klondike Kate, who carries the Klondike name on. Long may they all continue to delight us all.

27. Trip of a Lifetime

Mary Joynson

I didn't mean to cycle from Land's End to John O'Groats. I foolishly told a cycling friend that I'd always wanted to do it when I was younger, and before I'd fully realised what was happening, we were planning to do it together in 2014. She was celebrating her 60th birthday, and at 68 I was just hoping to keep up.

The plan was hatched at the end of 2013, at which time I was very unfit. I'd had a light year of cycling following a serious accident in 2012, so training began in earnest at the start of 2014. Everywhere I needed to go I tried to go by bike, trying to do 100 miles a week. We started to make detailed plans and I realised we'd have to do 60 or 70 miles *a day*! I increased the training. At the beginning of June we loaded our pannier bags onto the bikes and set off on the train bound for Penzance, full of trepidation.

When we left the station at Penzance and set off towards Land's End, I realised I'd made a Big Mistake. My companion (who was, and still is, very fit) rode away from me in the first mile of uphill! There was no way I could keep up. Mentally I started to make plans to crawl through Cornwall, Devon and Somerset and then catch the train at Bristol. That way, at least I could say I'd given it my best shot. While all this was going through my mind, I came to the top of the hill and started on a long descent. I don't think I'm reckless when descending, but I do like a bit of an adrenalin rush. Half way down I swept past my companion, descending slowly with the brakes on. Wow! I realised then that we could make it work. She'd be first to the top, I'd be first to the bottom. It just meant we wouldn't see much of each other.

We stayed overnight in a B&B in Penzance and set off north the following day. It was so hilly. I don't know how I got through the day – my legs hurt so much. The following morning I was amazed to find I could still walk, so gamely set off again. We were delighted to get out of Cornwall, but then found the hills of Devon even worse. To add to the problems, we were soaked to the skin in a really heavy thunderstorm that lasted a couple of hours. As soon as we'd dried off the rain started again and we were soaked for a second time. I was not happy. I was dreaming of Bristol railway station!

On the third day everything changed. My legs gave up protesting, we left Devon and rode down onto the Somerset Levels, the sun shone a bit and life seemed good. By the time we reached Bristol on the following day, all thoughts of Bristol railway station had gone from my head, and we rode triumphantly across the Severn Bridge into Wales, the first 'leg' of our journey behind us.

The next few days we rode up the beautiful Welsh border country and eventually arrived in Cheshire – the closest point to home. On a drizzly Sunday morning we met family and friends for coffee at a garden centre. So many people came to cheer us on and support us! We were very touched. It turned into quite a party, and at 11.30 we had to tear ourselves away.

We continued north, but now getting further away from home each day instead of closer. We wriggled our way around greater Manchester, keeping to lanes as much as we could, eventually reaching Kendal - the half way point. From there, over the Kirkstone Pass, through Carlisle and on into Scotland. We followed the west coast as far as Fort William, up the Great Glen to Inverness and then up the east coast all the way to John O'Groats. 17 days after having our pictures taken at the LE signpost, we posed again in front of the JOG signpost, 1030 miles behind us. I can honestly say, no one was more surprised than me.

But the biggest surprise was when the lady who kept the B&B where we'd stayed the night before, arrived at the signpost just as we were having our pictures taken. "Oh" she said "You've beaten me! I couldn't bear to think you'd ridden all this way and nobody here to greet you, so I've rushed through my jobs and was hoping to get here before you. Never mind, let's go in the café – lunch is on me!" And so saying she marched into the café and treated us to lunch. What a star!

I'm so pleased I allowed myself to be talked into doing something against my better judgement. What a wonderful trip. I'll never forget it. Oh, and not one puncture between us.

'Summer cycling' reproduced with permission of Dave Flitcroft – Artfromthebikeshed

Tutus, tears, and the awful tiger costume

Becky Latham

Becky is a student at Stoke-on-Trent Sixth Form College. In July 2016 she spent a week doing work experience with Cox Bank Publishing. She was inspired by some of the stories she read to write her own 'sporting story' about dance - and what a beautifully written story it is.

When I was only two and a half, my mum decided to enrol me into ballet and tap lessons at the Jill Clewes Performing Arts Centre to give me a hobby - and probably also because I was a very chubby baby. Most children lose interest in their first hobbies until they find what suits them best, switching between musical instruments or sporting activities, but surprisingly I maintained dance for a while. Until now, in fact, at seventeen years old.

There's something about my dance school which feels like a family. You see the same faces every week and it is a great space to build relationships. Dance teachers become like parental figures who teach you so much more than just dance, and even the other parents become like distant aunties and uncles. It really is a big community. I took a break during my GCSE exam period and returning again felt like going home.

Taking part in dance shows at the Regent Theatre will always hold some of my most treasured memories. Preparation begins around nine months prior to show week, which starts with extreme excitement but after a while becomes exhausting when the thrill has settled. Long Sundays are then spent sweating to perfect every move so you aren't the one to let the rest of the group down. However, the arrival of costumes usually sparks up interest again - whether that's a good thing or bad. Usually ballet costumes are pretty, a safe bet. The opening number costume is bound to be bright and loud, so you know what you're expecting. From there, it's all a game of luck and occasionally you do get an awful outfit.

I recall a fire drill happening on a dress rehearsal one year and my eleven-year-old self, whilst being led out of the building, wished it wasn't just before the *Pirates of the Caribbean* dance so my ugly pirate costume would be the one to burn in the flames. At that age I just wanted to wear pretty dresses and tutus (if I'm honest, I still do). The next show, when I was about thirteen, I got given a tiger print catsuit to wear in the circus dance which clung to me like a second skin. Most thirteen-year-olds do not appreciate being a tiger. Or being suffocated by lycra. As you can imagine, this did not make me a very happy thirteen-year-old.

Show week was always mad. The rush to find someone who could French plait your hair before it all started; the fight for mirrors to touch up the brightest red lipstick you owned; the distress when your costume disappeared from the rail and the rest of the room looked like a glittery, feathery mess. Infamous "Quick changes" were the worst, flinging your clothes around to find a crucial headpiece under the clutter as you could hear the current show number coming to an end. If you tell people you've been cursed with a "quick change" on the show schedule I guarantee you'll be met with a mournful look of condolence, paired with a brave pat on the back. *It was nice knowing you. Soldier on.*

But other than chaos, which is indeed part of the fun, there is nothing better than the exhilaration you get from performing on stage. Showing off the dances you spent long, hot days working over and missing events for is so fulfilling, but on the closing night it's bittersweet. Normally the show is held before the summer, and everyone is aware of the dancers who will soon be heading off to university and not perform with the dance school again. There's usually tears at that part. The shared emotion of happiness and sadness is also familiar because the show is over and done so quickly but all the sacrifices become worth it. It's only a two year wait until the next one.

I could write so much more about dance exams, classes and daily experiences which dance has helped to aid me through, but we would be here for centuries. I owe my sport a lot. It has helped my confidence, social skills, comfortability in my own body and provided me with friendships and memories which will remain with me until the day I die. Overall, I am who I am because of dance and the little community I have grown up in. Therefore, I am very grateful that, at the age of two and a half, my mum decided to take her chubby little child to learn to dance because I can confidently say it has been the best decision ever made in my life.

Becky with local designer and entrepreneur Andy Cooke,
in front of the City of Sport mural in Cheapside, Hanley

29. Fresh Air for Body and Soul

Maurice Leyland

Maurice is a local poet who we came across at a meeting of the Stoke Poetry Stanza, in the Leopard Inn in Burslem. He happened to read this new poem out that evening and we're delighted that he's given us permission to reproduce it here.

To walk the mountains helps to make me whole,
shakes off the dust of daily work and strain,
invigorates my body and my soul.
My muscles and my sinews learn again
To work, obey demands not made this week
nor many weeks before. My tired eyes
relearn what joys enfold – look and seek
what lies beyond, a new and glittering prize.

Take pride in memories of old, and tell:
The toil to conquer Crinkle Crags and back;
The blinding blizzard on Helvellyn top's hell;
The Snowdon summit reached by grim Pyg Track.
Forget what's past, discover paths anew.
Fulfil the needs of limbs and your heart too.

Fresh air for body and soul and paths anew: Great Gable in the Lake District

30. The 'Arf of Two 'Arfs!

Nicola Lingley-Heath

We had a number of projects running in the Stoke-on-Trent area through 2016, one of which was to produce a book on the City's iconic half marathon, the Potters 'Arf. We've had some great stories from the event, from runners, marshals, volunteers, organisers, sponsors and others. Thanks to Nicola for allowing us to share her story more widely - it's a real lesson in battling through difficulties and not giving up.

Running has never come naturally to me, despite my will to try. My attempts started as a kid during Primary School, where I had a go at joining the after-school cross country club. I turned up, nervous, in my little black pumps, shiny blue shorts and white T-shirt. I felt ready. Cross country was slower than sprinting, so surely I'd be ok at this. How wrong could I be?! It seemed all the sporty people were also good at this and I immediately fell to the back of the group. I was embarrassed and made to feel upset and rubbish at all the other kids jibes at the 'fat kid having a go'. I never went back! That after-school cross country session was a defining moment for me that put me off PE for the rest of my school years. I alternated between a verruca and being on my period every week, for the whole five years of high school. Embarrassed about taking part in athletics in front of the lads, nervous about being put on and being the let down in the 'good' team in rounders! I couldn't stand the thought of it, so avoided it like the plague.

Over the years, my weight increased bit by bit. By 2011, I saw a photo of myself and realised something had to change. After a couple of years of trying out various exercise classes, I had a moment of madness in 2013, when I signed up to the Greater Manchester

10k. Having never tried running again, since that after school club disappointment, I was taking a major step. I completed a *Couch to 5k* on the treadmill. To cut a long story short (there is more detail of this on my blog), it wasn't until 2015 that I completed my beginners course and joined Warrington Running Club. Over the past 16 months, I have gone from being a non-runner, unable to do a mile without stopping, to someone having done five half marathons, numerous 10ks and 5ks and, as of today, shortly about to take on the challenge of a marathon.

Potters 'Arf marathon. The event I have been wishing for for three whole years. After doing my beginners course in February 2015, I've spent every day following that working towards being able to do this race! I wanted to go 'home' and show all the people who laughed at the fat kid that I can do it, I have guts and determination, and can run a half marathon. For the whole week running up to the race, I prepared as well as I could have, ate well and drank plenty of water. I was so excited and looking forward to showing my mum and dad what I could do. Being Potters themselves and only living in Burslem, they were coming to see me off at the start line and wait around for me to cross the finish.

Arriving in Hanley early Sunday morning, I was filled with the feeling of familiarity. I haven't lived in Stoke for over 10 years but, despite a few changes in shop names, the town centre still looked the same. Having had my usual pre-race breakfast of porridge and bananas, I threw in some unconventionality, heading to the oatcake truck outside Boots! When in Stoke, you've got to have oatcakes, regardless of whether you're about to run 13.1 miles or not.

I was feeling so ready for this! I first considered the Potters 'Arf marathon after dabbling in running and completing the Manchester 10k in 2013. I struggled through that 10k using a run/walk method, and spent the whole time wishing I could be a 'proper' runner. I vowed to train harder for the following year and go back to run the race from start to finish. In 2014, I returned but sadly, I walked even more of the 10k than I had the previous year.

After trying all sorts of exercise classes and boot camps, I finally found a solution in February 2015. I enrolled myself on a beginners' running course! From the very first session, which saw me take tentative steps and barely manage a one-mile loop, I vowed that I'd work towards returning 'home' to do the Potters 'Arf!

Now here I was, 16 months and four half marathons later, stood on the start line with determination flowing through my veins. I was ready for this. I had my running buddies with me from my club back in Warrington (aka WRC) and felt like my head was completely in the zone. Even the rain hadn't put me off!

A couple of the guys from WRC had told me that the Potters 'Arf course was a toughie, with hills after hills and nowhere near as many downs as ups. Being a Stokie and growing up in the Potteries, I was fully aware of how hilly it is. Or so I thought!!

Pretty much as soon as we started there was a hill, and I realised I'd set off too fast to be able to maintain the pace for the whole distance, especially to combat the hills on route! For the time being, I went with the flow. It felt weird following the road round into the city centre. The route the 6a Bus went when I used to go 'up 'anley duck' as a teenager. Approaching the blue clock, an old school friend spotted me and shouted from the roadside, offering cheers and support. It set a whole bunch of butterflies floating round my belly with excitement and nerves about what I was about to take on. My head was in the game, my mind set was strong, I just hoped my body wouldn't let me down. The crowd-lined town centre was buzzing with claps and cheers from family, friends and passers-by as we ran past. Out of nowhere, I spotted my wife, mum and dad stood on the other side of the fence, cheering me on. It was just what I needed as the course seemed to open up before us and the Potters 'Arf really got going!

I felt good on my feet, distracted by the surroundings of my younger years. Passing Argos, where I used to spend many a weekend in the run up to Christmas, spending pocket money on gifts for my family, I was transported back to my youth, heading to the bus station after a hard day shopping in MarkOne and New Look. The only difference now is the bus station was on the opposite side of the road! It felt so strange, but oddly comforting. I started to settle into my stride, as we headed out towards Fenton.

Having been a student at Fenton Sixth Form, I knew there was a steady incline ahead. Memories flooded back to early mornings, having been on two bus journeys just to get to college, never mind starting the day. I thought back to how I dropped out after six months, never achieving my A Levels, at a loss as to where my life was heading; and then back to the present day, running past as a qualified nurse, having worked hard to get to this fantastic point in my life.

It gave me a boost and I plodded on up the hill. Almost immediately, I felt the burn in my calves, the tingle in my quads that comes with working the legs hard uphill and decided that, once I'd ran past Bryan Dale (the photographer I recognised from the Newcastle 10k), I'd have a little walk break to regain the feeling in my legs. I hadn't expected anything less knowing how friendly Stokies are, but I began to feel overwhelmed at all the car drivers shouting encouragement from their car windows; "go on duck, keep going"… "Well done duck, you're doing great"… It made me smile! They didn't seem fazed by the fact that they were stuck in a huge queue of traffic because of runners, like I've experienced many times in the past.

As I was catching my breath, my fellow WRCer Karen 'overtook' me. It was strange that we weren't running together, having spent all of our other races dragging each other round. This time, Karen knew I needed to do this race for myself, and she was quite happy with that. I was happy that she continued off in front of me too. It gave me something to chase and to focus on. I started up the plod again. I was shocked to see that I was still running ahead of my normal pace for a 10k let alone a half marathon. I was also shocked that I hadn't been passed by the pacer car…yet!

I could see the stream of bobbing heads up in front as we headed towards Longton. I still had my eye on Karen and felt comfy. As I was settling into the run, around 4-5 miles in, the pacer car came past me. It didn't perturb me as much as I thought it would and I just saw it as something else to chase. I managed to keep an eye on it in the distance but it seemed to edge further and further away as I headed up, what seemed like, a vertical road, to the top of a massively steep hill! It was actually quite tough to walk up it let alone run, but again the cheers and encouragement from spectators managed to pull me through the burning in my legs. By the time I reached the top, the pacer car had driven off into the distance, along with the other runners. I felt like I was running my own race, but still, the residents of the houses and the drivers in the cars continued to offer support.

Up to this point, around half way, I'd been having a fantastic run. I was running at a steady pace and was looking at a PB. How good would that have been…. A half marathon back on home turf and a PB to boot. Heading out of the estate I'd just run through, I struggled to identify which way I should have been going. All the other runners were out of sight and I couldn't see any marshals anywhere. I spotted an arrow on a lamppost which pointed to the left, directing me up another big hill. Going with the theme of the day, I plodded up the hill, feeling that something wasn't quite right but going with the flow. Further up the road (about half a mile according to my watch), two ladies pointed out to me that I was going the wrong way and needed to head back the way I'd come from. My heart sank! I could see the PB ticking away before my eyes…

In a bid to hold on to it, I upped the pace trying to catch up and regain my position back in the race. Knowing this could be the wrong thing to do, I took the chance. Unfortunately, it turned out as I expected, and the impact of me speeding up downhill to catch up, irritated a dormant injury that I've been trying to get over. My hips became niggly and I could feel muscles tightening up with every step. I had to revert to a run-walk to be able to continue. My chances at the PB were well and truly slipping away, along with my enthusiasm. My head was still in the game, but my body was letting me down. I'd prayed for a good run, knowing that my mum and dad were waiting for me at the end. I was so disappointed that I was now walking alone, miles away from the finish line. By mile 9, the tightness in my muscles had become so painful that I could barely walk let alone run. I considered ringing someone to come and collect me, but my determination and pride got the better of me. I'd got all the way to mile 9… Even if I walked the rest of the way, there was no way I was getting a DNF! I couldn't face the embarrassment! The Potters 'Arf 2016 was a relatively big deal to me and my family, and I didn't want to let anyone down.

I got my head down and tried to walk as fast as I could! Nothing was going to stop me reaching that finish line. Looking up to take a peek at whereabouts I was, I realised that Carmountside Crematorium was across the road. The wave of determination washed over me again, knowing that my great Auntie was over there. I whispered under my breath, 'this one's for you Auntie Helen'… Hoping she'd be watching over and give me a boost to the finish. I tried again to run a tree, walk a tree, but it was no good and the running had to give way to hobbling now.

Aside from the challenge of taking every step, the next big task upon me was that of 'Heartbreak Hill'. The warning 200m before the ascent would indicate to anyone that they should turn around and head in the opposite direction, but I had no choice but to plod on if I wanted to get to the finish line. A group of StokeFIT people were stood at the bottom of the hill cheering as loud as they could. I recognised Claire, a college friend of a fellow Stokie member of WRC - Nicola - and felt a huge amount of support from her and the rest of her squad of cheerers. I realised that Nic had caught up with me and was only a few strides behind. Although I'd vowed that this was a race I wanted to do for myself, I have to admit it was nice to have some company up the almost vertical climb, as Nic and I walked up the hill together.

Once at the top, another StokeFIT member ran with Nic to encourage her on to the finish, I cheered her on as she went off ahead. I wondered how well Antony, another WRC friend of mine had got on chasing a PB, and whether he'd managed to get it, knowing how tough the course had been. I then wondered how Karen had got on. My closest running buddy in terms of pace. I hoped she'd managed a good time and I wondered whether she'd have finished yet. My thoughts then turned to my family. I knew I only had just over a mile to go. I wondered if they thought I'd done rubbish, whether I'd been really slow and whether I shouldn't have bothered doing the race at all.

Nearing Hanley Forest Park, I knew the end was in touching distance, and I tried to focus on getting there, wincing through the pain of every step. I tried to keep myself together, focusing on the last three quarters of a mile. I fought back tears as every step got me closer to the finish line. I felt disappointed in my efforts of the second half of the race. As I approached the Potteries Centre, I knew the finish line was only a few hundred metres way, and I just tried to focus on moving my feet to get me across that line. Out of nowhere, I heard a familiar voice shout, 'you alright Stokie?'….it was my good mate Dave, Karen's other half, who'd driven all the way from Warrington just to support the gang! Stokie is my nick name amongst some of the members of our club and hearing the endearment behind the name unleashed the emotions I'd been trying so hard to hold back, flowing like a tidal wave! Tears rolled down my cheeks and I sobbed through broken sentences, explaining to Dave how much pain I was in and about not wanting to get a DNF, and how I felt I'd let everyone down. He took my hand and walked with me back into the town centre, past the remaining spectators clapping my efforts, past the blue clock, and into the last few metres of the course. The other WRCers had finished and were all cheering me on

with my wife, and stood next to them was my mum and dad. I saw, through tear clouded eyes, that they looked emotional too. I couldn't have been going any slower if I tried but I was in touching distance of the finish line. Nicola had just finished and was on the other side of the fence. She threw a load of encouragement at me and we exchanged a huge hug just before I edged towards the line. Dave had gone back to the cheer squad, Nic had gone to her family and I was alone, riding solo over that finish line! I'd done it! I'd done the Potters 'Arf marathon. I'd walked the last four miles, getting slower and slower, and my finishing photos weren't going to be pretty, but I'd done it.

The past three hours had been a test of my strength, my ability and my determination. It had been filled with ups and downs, and not just the hills. Three hours of memories of my life flashing before me, three hours of reflection on the person I've become and three hours of belly burning fire, getting me round the hardest race I've ever done, and to the finish line! I cried hard into my dad's shoulder, as he hugged me and cried too – with pride! Mum came along and we cried together too. To see them so proud of me for finishing a race is something I'll never forget. I was so overcome with emotion – relief, pride, happiness, pain! I wiped away the tears and hobbled through the finish funnel to my family and friends! I was in so much pain, but every step had been worth it.

At various points of the course, I'd thought to myself that I was going to give up running. Questioned whether I even enjoyed it. Now that it was all over, I knew that I'd be signing up to Potters 'Arf 2017. I might have finished this year, but I now have a massive score to settle with this course! I returned to my hometown to prove a point. That, I have done!

Next year, I'll be back to smash that 'point' to pieces, to make my mum and dad proud all over again.

HANLEY
The Hanley Building Society
Potters' 'Arf Marathon 2016
328

31. Charlie and the Karvan go to... Northwood Stadium

Peter Hooper

Wednesday 17th August 2016 saw a major Street Games festival at Northwood Stadium in Stoke-on-Trent. Fresh from our workshop success at Middleport (see page 41), Emma Dawson Varughese and I pitched up at Northwood with her trusty Karvan and gazebo for more story writing. This time we had artist Charlie Walker for the whole day, and he got some lovely portraits too.

Street Games is a charity aimed at making sport more accessible to disadvantaged children, and Stoke-on-Trent City Council has been involved in it from its earliest days, so it was great for the 2016 European City of Sport to be hosting the festival for 11-17 year olds – and for *Sporting Stories* to be part of it.

The weather on the day was perfect, so with no rain (just a lot of sun) our main challenges were (a) being located next to a huge inflatable assault course – a bit more of a draw than the lovely Karvan; and (b) being located some distance away from the burger van, another significant youth-magnet! Despite this, we had a steady stream of people coming to find out what we were doing, and got another suite of stories covering different activities. Charlie had a field day with his sketches and we found he was very good at chatting to his subjects and encouraging them get their stories down. This was something we exploited to its maximum at our next workshop event in Hanley (see page 227).

Here's a selection of what we collected at Northwood on the day:

Simple Fate – Kyle Onza

When I was 10 I started martial arts in Warrington. I loved it because I learned new techniques and I met my Sen Sai (*a martial art teacher or mentor*) at this club. My foster dad knew my Sen Sai from work and this is how I came to Atemi-Jujitsu. From the Warrington club we moved to Sutton leisure centre where I continued Atemi-Jujitsu but here I became a kind of teacher; I was teaching simple break-away techniques, block punches and simple throws as well. The kids I taught were about seven. But it was time to move again and the club moved down the road into its own premises. At this point I've got six years' experience in Atemi-Jujitsu.

We renovated this club that we call the "dojo", fitting, matting and decorating. My Sen Sai has employed instructors now so it's much busier than before, we even teach combatives – the kind of martial arts used in the Royal Marines. We also have Thai Boxing and a women's self-defence. I feel that my time at the martial arts centre has got me ready for a life in the army – both physically and mentally. I feel confident, determined and strong!

Coming Back – by Jay Sandhu

I've never been the best at sport, but always enjoyed playing: basketball, American football, football. I've always been the one that tries the hardest and never gives up!
Whilst at university I got involved in loads of sports – dodgeball, American football again and of course football. After numerous trials and much hard work I made it into the university football team: having thought I would not even make the second round of trials I was ecstatic to make the team.

It was all going well in training, played the first match, obviously put in a solid performance at right back, threatening on occasion. Put a few decent balls into the box, unfortunately the strikers didn't convert, but we did win in the end, 3-1. A direct free kick for the first; the left winger cut inside, put one top corner for the second. The opposition pulled one back after a scramble in the box led to a corner. We scored the final goal from a beautiful through ball to the striker who casually slotted the ball into the bottom corner. A great win for the lads!

Next training session spirits were high, morale was good. We started with basics and then got straight into a game. A ball was lofted from the opposition towards me, I jumped to win the ball (which of course I did!), went to lean on the other team's winger in the air but he hadn't jumped! As I landed my left foot planted me one way and my knee twisted the other.

"Pop"! My knee went. I was in agony, it ballooned and I could hardly move it. One of my mates said "Just walk it off, you'll be fine". I quickly shot back "Does your knee look like this, it's clearly not OK!". After five minutes or so I tried to walk/jog but couldn't at all. I had to hobble off and got picked up. I was distraught – I might not ever be able to play football again, devastated didn't even describe it.

After a few days the swelling reduced and I went to the hospital and they confirmed the worst – I'd torn my cruciate ligament! I honestly didn't know what to do with myself. Sport was my life. It was everything to me!

I got booked in for my op and started physio. I did at least three times more of each exercise I was given, I was determined to get back playing as soon as I could. I got a phone call from the hospital – I thought my op was pushed back but they said if I wanted it quicker I could go to a different hospital, I obviously said "Yes" straight away! When I was in hospital waiting I was nervous until I found out that I had the same surgeon as Michael Owen, I calmed down I was in good hands!

After the op I endured months of boring tedious recovery and tons of physio. It was horrible knowing all my mates were playing and I couldn't. When I was ready to play again, nearly twelve months after my injury I was ready to come back!

In my first game back everything seemed slower than I remember, I was buzzing to get back playing! Before I never scored or got near the goal. On this occasion I managed to break free heading towards the goal, screaming for the ball, my mate (usually a ball-greedy striker) played me the ball I was shocked and continued to gallop forward, when I got one-on-one my mind started to race where do I put my shot? How hard do I kick? How close do I get? How do I kick? Trying to analyse the keeper's movements... then I had to stop thinking and just shoot! I can't even remember how but the ball was in the back of the net, I wheeled off in celebration I was ecstatic! Celebrated with my team, it felt great.
I was back!

Football - Josh Hampton

My name is Josh Hampton, I play football at Northwood Stadium on Wednesday with my carer. I enjoy football and love scoring goals especially with my head. My best foot is my left foot and I've scored many goals with it from corners.

I love Stoke City the football club. I go and watch the team when I can and scream when I can to encourage them to perform better. I love mountain walking and getting to great heights, being on top of the clouds.

Danny Hannan.

I am Josh's carer and take Josh on many activities including football and walking. We play at Northwood Stadium on Wednesday when I look after him. Recently we had a camping trip to the Lake District where we climbed Helvellyn which was an outstanding achievement. For him we plan to do more walking and plan to climb Scafell Pike really soon.

Canoeing – Tayibah

Today was amazing we did canoeing. I did it with Safa. She was really scared she was screaming. She did not paddle properly. But it was not her fault, the water was really heavy. We were hitting the wall a lot. The man Wilson was really fun, he was splashing us.

Canoeing – Safa

Today was a great experience because we went canoeing and it was a bit scary because we bumped into a few things like river banks and bushes and stuff. Lots of different people were walking past and we were greeting them. Hello ☺ Also we were splashing water at each other's faces with the paddles.

Images of writers at the Street Games Festival – courtesy of artist Charlie Walker

32. Sailing

Sophie Longmore

I can see them out there. Carefree and nothing to worry about. Then the wind picks up and they lean out. Heads nearly touching the water. I watch as he carefully moves the rudder into the wind to perform his tack. So graceful, yet so strong. The wind seems to throw the boat around, however the sailor just leans out, putting all his trust in the foot straps, and takes back control. The passion. The understanding. The sailor and the boat become one. I love it.

It isn't as easy as I'd first imagined. Even getting into the wetsuit is hard. It seems to stick to my skin. It doesn't help that it is a winter one so it is that much thicker. When I finally get this second skin on I feel like I might explode. Oh well, at least I'll be warm.

When I finally get to the lake I see how hard it is. I tack and duck, but don't duck low enough. The boom swings and hits me. Why is sailing so dangerous? Then I fall. Down I go. Splash! I swallow half the lake as I capsize. I give up, I will never do this right. I start to pull my boat back to shore but then Steph comes out and asks me what I am doing. Like the coach she is she picks me up and gets me going again. Red buoy, green buoy, blue buoy, again and again. I tack and it works, finally I begin to enjoy it. I am on top of the world.

When I get to the changing room the wetsuit just falls off. As I wash away the dirt and grime I feel so alive, I did it. When I go into the room Steph is there. She hands me an envelope. Grade 1 sailing complete. My life is complete!

33. The Stoke-on-Trent Triathlon

Gianni Loska

It's that time again. When you wake up feeling the same nerves as any other competition day. But something about today felt different. Maybe waking up at 5am. Or maybe it was that I was going to Trentham Gardens. Not on a school walk this time but to do a triathlon. When we arrived I unloaded my bike from the back of my Dad's van. Took my kit bag and went to get signed in. After we had received our race number I went to put my bike in transition. I was in space 116 as that was my race number.

I then went for a warm up and jogged around the bike and run course. After that we were called up to Trentham Lake for race briefing and the start. We had to do a 50m swim in open water in Trentham Lake. Then we cycled 5km on a grass course which I did on my mountain bike. Finally a 2.5km grass run around Trentham Gardens. But because of health and safety we had to start 10 seconds apart from each other. It went in number order starting at 1.

When it was your turn you all lined up on the pontoon and waited for the starter to set you. You dived off the pontoon and into the freezing cold lake. I wore a triathlon suit but some people wore wetsuits but my friend wore swimming trunks and a swim shirt. You had to swim around three triangular buoys, which were set out in a triangular course. You had to do two laps of the course which gave you a 50m swim. You then got out of the water, ran along the pontoon, put your trainers on and took the 800m run to transition. When I arrived in transition my hands were still cold so it was hard to put my helmet on. But I did it and started the bike course. We had to do two laps of a 2.5km course which was set on grass. For me it was too short so I just sprinted it.

I just jumped off my bike and ran it into transition, hooked it up on the rack, took my helmet off and headed out on the run course. It was a 2.5km run around Trentham Gardens. We had to do two laps. It felt like a cross-country race! I sprinted through the finish but you didn't know your time until it got put on the UK Triathlon website a few hours after the race.

When we were eating dinner at home I got an email and I found out I won! I was ecstatic! I was the quickest child in the 9-12 year-old category!

34. My Sporting Story

Janet Mason

When I was at grammar school in the 1960s, I loved all sport. I was strong, with lots of energy, and as they say, it was a 'no-brainer' that I would be involved in every sport going. In an all girls school, it was so easy to take every opportunity offered. We hardly had any male teachers and certainly not for PE. It's funny but I don't remember any of the PE teachers but I do remember loving being part of a team. I was goal attack in the netball team and played in all the matches. I was in the hockey team too... I liked that less because I'm not fond of being hit on the shins with a hockey stick. Whoever invented that game was a sadist.

I loved long jump, high jump, javelin and shot put. I competed in County games and loved going to different venues. I was a working class kid who never went anywhere so it was very exciting to me. I suppose it all ended when I had to get a Saturday job but I don't remember consciously making that choice. It's a good job my best mate then, is my best mate still, and 50 years later I can still tap into our shared memories of school. Both of us loved sport and the opportunities it opened up for us.

For a long time after school I never thought of sport... too busy as a far-too-young mother... to participate in such trivia. That's the way I would have described it... if anyone had asked... but of course they didn’t.

I went to University as a mature student... lol... I was 27... and I started to play squash. That was as scary as hockey. I didn't like the aggression it brought out in my partners.

There were definitely sports clubs advertising on fresher's week but I was a single mother of two and they were clearly not for me. As a so-called mature student, we weren't exactly welcome in 1977. There was a big Student Union building and a little hut for mature students. Yeah, we knew our place.

Work, work and more work kept sport at bay. I always liked to be fit and healthy; and swimming was my chosen activity... alone... as a detox... an antidote to stress. It would never have occurred to me to get involved in sport. As a woman, I thought sport equalled all things masculine and competition equalled aggression.

When at last, I had time to spare, at 57, having accepted voluntary redundancy, I saw an article in the Evening Sentinel about an Outrigger group on Trentham Lake. I contacted them without hesitation and became a member. Seven years later I became the Secretary of the newly formed Outrigger Club and here I am two years later; out on the lake five times a week and enjoying every moment.

I don't think of it as a sport because it's a sociable, cooperative activity which attracts as many women as men... maybe more; and it constantly surprises us, as women, that it's seen by others as a bit 'brave'. It's so easy and not at all scary. It's good for the bingo wings and it's a great opportunity to get away from the stresses of everyday life and to be more mindful of nature. It's not an enormous lake but it has everything we need and we are out in all weathers, determined to cast off the mantle of 'wimp'! What fun! It's filled a huge gap in my life and many of our 60 members would say the same thing. I think that, for me as a woman it's the opportunity to stop multi-tasking and to focus on what's important: friendship, teamwork, fitness, and nature.

I'd like to think that all children, and especially, young people, could be encouraged to get involved, and stay involved, in a variety of activities which could be re-named anything but 'SPORT'!

35. "You Should Be Dead"

Nigel Moore

I'm a member of Lyme Racing Club and I race cross country mountain bike races. On the morning of October 4th 2012 I told my wife Alison that I was nipping out for a quick training ride and I would be back in a couple of hours and, as it was a nice day, we could nip to Blackpool for a fish and chip supper ... but I never made it home.

Halfway round the ride there's a ledge, with a 60ft drop to the left, that I needed to negotiate. Just as I arrived there was a squirrel on the trail so I decided to stop, still clipped in, and lean on a post to wait for the squirrel to move. When it did I pushed off but with too much force and then my world started to go very wrong.

I began to fall down the cliff, I hit a tree half way down thinking, "If I live I'm going to be paralysed," then I smashed into the ground between two big rocks. My first thought was, "Thirty seconds of intense pain then it'll be all over," so I said "Love you Ali, bye," but nothing happened, so I gingerly wiggled my toes and realised I wasn't paralysed. However I knew from the pain I was in serious trouble so I searched for my phone, which was in an inside pocket, in my jacket and that's when I realised I couldn't see my left arm... It was behind my back.

To cut a long story short, I managed to phone emergency services who airlifted me to hospital where I was told the extent of my injuries - which were life threatening. I had nine broken ribs, both lungs were punctured and my left one had collapsed - and my left arm was dislocated coming to rest behind my back. The whole extent of my injuries were summed up by a surgeon a week later, "Sit down Mr Moore, I want to shake your hand."

"Why's that doctor?" I replied … to which he said "I've just read your notes; you should be dead."

I was told I'd spend five weeks in hospital and I would have six months off work and even longer off the bike. However, I didn't see that as an option. So after five days I asked my surgeon to take my chest drain out so I could go home. He said that my fitness and my resilience to pain would allow me to go home just so long as I followed his advice completely and carried on taking my morphine. Not taking the morphine wasn't an option; the pain was excruciating. I could hardly walk, I couldn't wash myself, I couldn't even go to the toilet on my own and I had little or no sleep for three weeks, but I was determined to get back to training as soon as possible so I endured all the hardships knowing that my wife and I had booked a training holiday - for the end of February - before I had my accident.

Come February we went away and I started training and amazingly my physical fitness wasn't as dire as I thought it might be but my psychological fitness was in a very bad place and what worried me more was I was on a road bike not a mountain bike. However, I shrugged it off and continued training: I had a Nationals at Margam Park to train for.

My fitness improved and come the day of the Nationals I felt confident. Foolishly I decided not to do a recon lap, so when the gun went on the start I raced up the first climb reaching the top of the first descent in 5th place but then my world imploded. I was totally overwhelmed by fear, reduced to tears and unable to complete even one lap. Back home my wife and I sat down and reviewed my progress to date and what I wanted to do and the conclusion my awesome wife came to was that I needed to "grow a pair."

Nearly four years on I'm still a work in progress, but I'm actually a better, more skilled, fitter rider still trying to regain my previous results and I'm convinced at some point I will be rewarded for all my hard work, though it would be nice to have a better bike so I didn't have to work quite so hard.

36. The Lord Mayor's Sporting Story

Anthony Munday, Lord Mayor of Stoke-on-Trent

I've been a sports enthusiast ever since I was a small boy, so it should not come as a surprise there will be a sporting theme running throughout my year (2016/17) as Lord Mayor. Stoke-on-Trent's status as European City of Sport gave me even more of an excuse to do so and I've unashamedly, and justifiably in my opinion, used that excuse to its full extent.

When we read a newspaper or watch the television, it seems hardly a day or two goes by before the subject of obesity in one form or other is high on the agenda. We are told the number of children who are diagnosed with Type 2 diabetes, which was a rare occurrence not too many years ago, is on a rapid rise and the consequence will be a massive strain on the National Health Service. No, we don't need a rocket scientist to conclude we need to encourage as many people as possible, of all ages and including primary school children where the issue is particularly serious, to take up some form of regular exercise.

Inevitably, times change and we live in a far different world than when I left school 40 years ago. When I grew up, there were no games consoles, i-Phones or other devices to compete with football, cricket and other sports and outdoor pursuits. Of course today's devices provide terrific entertainment and computers make our lives much easier in many ways, which is great, but it is far from great when sport and other healthy activities are pushed down the pecking order.

From as early as I can remember, my favourite sport was football. Me and my friends played in the school playground, on any patch of spare ground we could find after school and on the community centre ground on the border of Baddeley Green and Stockton Brook on Sunday afternoons. There was often 20-a-side at 'The Com' with the big boys joining in.

I played for the school team in my last two years at Greenways Primary, where we had a very good side the first year but not so good the next, but I wasn't good enough to play for the team at Holden Lane High School. Managed by PE master Neil Gilson, Holden Lane had a fantastic team with many of the players signing for Stoke City and Port Vale as 16-year-olds, although only left-back Paul Johnson went on to enjoy a useful professional career with Stoke and Shrewsbury Town.

After leaving school I played for numerous Baddeley Green-based sides, on Saturdays and Sundays, in the local senior leagues and won a few trophies here and there before suffering a compound fracture of my right leg at the age of 26.

I was playing for Bennett's pub at Cobridge on the football pitch adjoining what was once the resplendent Sneyd Cricket Ground. It was a Potteries & District League Division One fixture against Dresden Nomads and the game was abandoned while we waited for the ambulance. At one stage it was feared I might lose my leg below the knee, but thankfully I managed to recover, although not well enough to play football at a competitive level again.

I ran a couple of Potteries Marathons when I was still playing football, with a best time of three hours and 26 minutes in 1984, and was able to take up running after recovering from my broken leg.

Eventually, when I was in my late 30s, my old football injuries struggled to cope with the strain of running and I took up cycling. I've never attempted to cycle competitively, choosing to buy a hybrid bike to climb the hills and see the magnificent countryside in a 25-mile radius about the area I live.

I still cycle regularly today and have completed a couple of coast to coast challenges in recent years, the latest in July (Silloth to Tynemouth) when four of my friends joined me as we raised almost £5,000 for the Lord Mayor's Charities – the North Staffs Heart Committee, the Sir Stanley Matthews Coaching Foundation and the Macari Foundation for homeless people. A Lord Mayor's Golf Day followed in September, with 76 players taking part and another £1,200 raised, and I plan to end my Mayoral year with another sporting event which just about everyone will be able to take part in. That event is still in the planning stage.

Of course any form of exercise is good for you and we are all told a brisk walk for 30 minutes, three or four times per week, is as good as anything. I believe everyone who is able to should try to exercise, for their own health and also to ease the burden on our NHS, which for all its problems still provides a fantastic service far more often than not.

The Lord Mayor's Golf Day, with Lord Mayor Anthony Munday (front) and (left to right) John Farmer (general manager at Trentham Park Golf Club); John Rudge (former Port Vale manager and Stoke City Coach); and Phil Sproson (former Port Vale centre-back).

37. City of Sport 2016

Frank Murphy

Frank Murphy is the co-founder of StokeFIT running club, which was established in 2012. FIT stands for ***F****riends* ***I****n* ***T****raining – and the club is exactly that, wonderfully inclusive and hugely popular. He is also the winner of Run Leader of the Year 2015; and 2016 Coach of the Year at the Stoke-on-Trent Sports Personality of the Year Awards. He wrote this very powerful blog at the time that Stoke-on-Trent was announced as European City of Sport.*

- *Nothing to do.*
- *Crack head central.*
- *Complete sh*t hole.*

- *Opportunity, character, home*
- *On the change.*
- *Unaware of potential.*

The six statements above came in reply to a request I put out on Facebook to "describe Stoke-on-Trent in three words". I got other answers, but I chose the above because they're the most striking and definitive.

The first three came from people not regularly actively involved in sport. The latter three came from people who regularly take part in sport.

The six statements, and many of the others, reaffirm my claim that being an active participant in sport positively affects other aspects of your lifestyle, and your outlook on life, whilst non-participation is equally detrimental to your attitude and outlook on life.

Now, I've just returned home from the launch event naming Stoke-on-Trent, our great city, as the 'European City of Sport'. This is literally, a once per generation event, where our city has been recognised and regarded as the city with the most sporting potential of all other cities across Europe. This award, this recognition; because that's what it is, puts our city on a par with past winners of the award such as Madrid, Dublin, Rotterdam, Copenhagen, Milan and Marseille. It's not a sympathy vote; it's not a bid to help us. It's 100% recognition of our city and our people and the potential that is held within each of us proud Stokies.

People from all around the world recognise that you and I are capable of whatever we want to be capable of. They recognise that our children, the future of our city, have massive massive potential, and they want to back us. So now it's time to step up. We need to unite together and become a city full of doers. We need to make 2016 THE year for sport in our city. It's our time to showcase ourselves to the rest of the world. It's our chance to prove to the world that there IS plenty to do in our home town. We need to show the world, that we're not crack heads and that we're capable and willing of looking after the people in our city that need help.

We need every single person in Stoke-on-Trent to play their part in showing that we live in a beautiful, bustling, lively city, and not a complete sh*t hole. To make 2016 work properly, we need everybody to be inspired to be active in sports, any sports. Regularly. We need to remove stigmas, banish labels. We need to inspire. Motivate. Generate.

We need players, jumpers, runners, players, swimmers, climbers, riders, throwers, cheerers, clappers, helpers, supporters.

Most of all we need tryers.

We need people, every person, to go out and try something new. To take a friend. To stand in the rain whilst their children try a new sport. We need you, to be brave, to make a change, to have a go, to be proud, to enjoy.

We need the children of our city to see their parents make being active a part of normal life. We need to develop a drive and determination in our children; our future to get out and try. To push themselves, to approach new sports and activities.

None of this will come without conscious effort by you and me. We need to show Stoke-on-Trent that there is nothing wrong with being new to something. We need to become facilitators. We need to go out of our way.

Changing our attitude to helping people change will change lives. It will create lives. It will change attitudes. It will create a city to be prouder of. It will create a city to aspire to. Do it now. Plan, inspire, develop, play, cheer, encourage, motivate.

My three words to describe our home:

- *Concentrated*
- *Undiscovered*
- *Potential.*

38. I Love My Sport... with Trentham Outrigger Club

Gilbert Owen

Many thanks to Janet Mason (see her story on page 162), secretary of the Trentham Outrigger club, for submitting this wonderful story from Gilbert Owen. Stoke-on-Trent is certainly blessed with some inspirational octogenarians!

I'm 80 years old now and fit as a fiddle! How have I maintained my level of health and fitness? Well, it's a long story... a lifetime of perseverance really.

I left school in 1950 and by 1951 I was boating most weekends on Longton Park lake and that's when I met my wife to be. I managed to persuade her to get into my little rowing boat and we never looked back... Was I a good catch? Well, I was an apprentice with Stoke City Council and exempt from National Service because of that... so maybe there was a shortage of lads available for courting... At the tender age of 21, I was conscripted into the Highland Light Infantry, spending my time in Cyprus and Germany. Kathleen wrote to me and after three years I came home and we married in 1957.

We had a happy married life and when Kathleen died I found myself at a bit of a loose end... aged 72, still working... part time at Wedgwood Memorial College... I needed an extra hobby. Kathleen had never wanted to dance... and had no interest in cruises. Now I was able to embark (no pun intended) on two new hobbies which would combine in a very satisfying way...

I went on my first cruise at 72... to Spain and Portugal... and met up with a guy who had also lost his wife. I decided, 'if I'm cruising; I need to get dancing!'

On my return, I enrolled with the U3A... Stone branch... and struggled greatly for the first 8 or 9 months... to learn the Cha Cha; the Rumba; the Foxtrot; Waltz; and Quick Step. I suppose it helped that I have always kept fit... swimming, walking with the Ramblers, table tennis, and of course, always working; but honestly, there were times when I thought I'd never be a dancer! I'm not one to give up though; and the company of other like-minded older people in the U3A really helped me.

I heard about a group who were enjoying paddling on Trentham Lake in a weekly session organised by ex-Olympic canoeist John Court under the auspices of Stone U3A. Just my cup of tea I thought, and joined up. After all, I was only 76, and not the oldest member. I discovered quite quickly that I have an aptitude for steering and I think I've been a useful asset!

My confidence was boosted and when I saw an advert for 'Dance Afloat' based in Ipswich; straightaway I applied to be a volunteer dance host with a variety of cruise ships. I've worked on 27 cruises now and have visited so many countries including Australia, Vietnam, the Caribbean, Iceland, Spain, the Baltic, the Rhine and Kiel Canal, as well as the British Isles. It's a fantastic hobby and I get to practice my dance steps with a huge variety of partners all expenses paid! Can't be bad!

I firmly believe that as you get older, you have to keep yourself fit and push yourself. Steering the Outrigger canoes is harder than it looks but like anything else, practice makes perfect. I'm not one to blow my own trumpet but I'm happy to share my experiences with others... if it's useful.

During the last couple of years, we have been extending the membership of the Outrigger Club and I have been able to assist in that by sharing my skills and being available (when not cruising!) to help our new members... male and female... to master the art of steering. The lake can be a windswept cold place and as I said, it takes some hard work and perseverance to steer well. I take part in three sessions a week now and totally enjoy the experience. We are able to keep an eye on the wildlife... close up... and often have the extra bonus of catching sight of the kingfishers and rare red-necked grebes.

I suppose I'm lucky to be so fit and healthy but I feel very strongly that we are able to add to our fitness at any point in our lives... and if you choose to be a couch potato you'll definitely get your chips... pun fully intended...

Gilbert and the Trentham Outriggers – photo courtesy of Janet Mason

39. What Sport Means To Me

Jonathan Pace

Jonathan is Head of Sports Development & Active Lifestyles at Staffordshire University – and tells us here what sport means to him...

HAVING been asked to write a piece on the *City of Sport* for The Sentinel, I immediately phoned my dad.

I tend to share all of my good news stories with him. I also tend to use it as a way of showing off. My dad is, you see, a massive local sports supporter, and has been all his life.
In my role I get to meet people who, in his younger years, he used to watch and follow with great admiration.

Phoning him to tell him I was sat with Sir Stanley Matthews's daughter, the inspirational Jean Gough, looking through Sir Stan's family photo album for images to use in our newly refurbished Sir Stanley Matthews Sports Centre here at Staffordshire University is still my highlight.

Putting him on the phone to Gordon Banks or having my picture taken with Terry Conroy still makes a bloke in his mid-70s fill with pride (and more than a little envy).

Why am I telling you this? Well on Mother's Day it finally happened. I had been using my parents as the ultimate barometer for the impact of Stoke-on-Trent becoming a European City of Sport. In their 70s, active in terms of they walk wherever and whenever they can, but the opportunity that caught my dad's eye was the sharing of sporting stories, and he has a few I can tell you.

This filled me with enthusiasm, ECoS2016 will impact a real cross-section of people from all over our wonderful city. Whether it's becoming more active, physically and mentally, or sharing one of thousands of great sporting stories generated across the Potteries, this is a real positive.

Throughout the year, and beyond into the future, Stoke-on-Trent being a European City of Sport will help to deliver a number of sports and healthy lifestyle activities, providing an opportunity for everyone to improve the general health and wellbeing of our city.

All the great sports stories aside, we do unfortunately have a very inactive population. Some of the initiatives will no doubt help to reduce the barriers folks have with accessing activities – cost and time – with many free and reduced price activities spread across all manner of times and venues.

But this needs to be a city-wide effort to spread the word about the benefits of a healthier lifestyle.

We have some wonderful green space across the area, fantastic connections via the canals and greenways, linking the city together. There is no charge for their access (maybe some bread for the ducks) they have longer opening times than the shops, and give you great access to some of the more forgotten parts of our little piece of the world. I haven't come across a local sports club that doesn't throw its doors open to potential new members.

I've been lucky enough to play a small part in helping to bring one of the most accessible, family friendly, welcoming activities the city has in parkrun, showing the way a community of like-minded volunteers can develop a project that positively impacts on the health of the city, averaging almost 200 participants on a weekly basis. I remember setting the course out on the first day, getting 14 people and being pleased that someone turned up.

I'm very lucky in my role, as I'm surrounded by the positivity of sport and physical activity on a daily basis.

I see students, staff and the local community engaging in all aspects of sport and fitness on our university campus, from recreational Glow in the Dark Badminton (yes it's a thing), to our competitive Team Staffs clubs and beyond into working with some really talented students through our Elite Athlete Program.

It is this daily connection with sport and physical activity that makes me realise what a positive impact the European City of Sport can have, but the word needs spreading to everyone, by everyone.

So that brings me back to my parents. They aren't on Twitter surprisingly, or Facebook, but they are now telling all their friends about the fact that we are a European City of Sport and that, in lots of small ways, we can all improve the health of our city. We can all become ambassadors, so let's make the most of this opportunity. After all, Stoke-on-Trent is definitely on the up.

If you love sport, then why not tell the world what you love about it and why?

Write a *Sporting Story*...

Thanks to Jonathan and the Sentinel for allowing this article to be republished here.

40. parkrun: Celebrating in the Rain

Ruth Parsons

In a book full of inspiring individuals with wonderful sporting stories to tell, it's impossible to pick out particular stars, but if I had to then Ruth is up there with the best of them. This little piece of writing is about mental strength, physical toughness, club running, the parkrun community at its finest, and more.

It was a soggy morning, with no hope of it brightening up anytime soon, but dedicated individuals pulled on their trainers, grabbed their barcodes, and headed to the park (bandstand where it was dry!) ready for 9.00 am start. For most, it was just another ordinary Saturday at parkrun, some ready and raring for a PB, first-timers, and others just happy to have a gentle jog with friends.

But it was no ordinary day for me; in fact it was somewhat a special day, even if I had brought my bad luck with me in the form of rain! It was three years to the day that I was sat in the emergency assessment bay in the Cancer Centre at UHNM being told I had a rare form of blood cancer, Chronic Myeloid Leukaemia. I can't say it has been an easy journey, and it still isn't over, but I know from the bottom of my heart I would've never started running if it wasn't for the diagnosis.

I would never have one day - tired, sick, in pain and weak - have decided to put my trainers on and run down the road. I would never have built it up to one mile, then two, then a 5k, then Alsager 5, then joining Newcastle (Staffs) A.C, then a 10k, then eight half marathons and now in the last few weeks of training for the 2016 London Marathon (running for the Teenage Cancer Trust).

I would never have the friends I've made, the laughter, support, encouragement, inspiration and drive in life without running. I'd like to thank everyone that's joined me from the start, along the way, and right up to Saturday on my three year cancerversary, where we ran, chatted and laughed our way around the 5k, followed by cake, hugs and smiles!

Ruth at the 2016 Potters 'Arf – one of the toughest half marathon courses in the UK. This after completing the 2016 London Marathon, and three weeks before she went on to complete the Potteries Marathon – reputedly the seventh hilliest marathon course in the world. Photo courtesy Mick Hall.

41. Like Paddling Through Your Own Wildlife Documentary

Zoe Robinson

Stoke-on-Trent is not the most obvious place to live and to take up a new activity based entirely on the sea. But, after many years of different sports, sea kayaking is now what I 'do', and I'm pretty sure it's here to stay. Sea kayaking can involve a lot of time moving slowly, through a salty landscape giving plenty of time to think, and I have spent a lot of time thinking about why I sea kayak. Each weekend I drive to Anglesey in North Wales. It has done terrible things to my carbon footprint which sits uncomfortably with me. So why do I sea kayak? Here are some of the top things it has given me.

Number 1. It is like living in your very own wildlife documentary. I used to spend a lot of time hillwalking. I've done much less of this recently, spending much more of my time at sea level. When I recently returned to the hills (an amazing trip in itself, with my first solo Munros (Scottish hills over 3000 feet), my first Munros by train, and my first solo wild camp), one of the things that struck me is how 'dead' the hills seemed compared to the sea. Just getting the train back along the coast, I saw more wildlife than I had in three days living and walking in the hills. Almost every sea paddle I have ever done I have seen seals, sometimes surfing a wave alongside me, following the sea kayak in the water, and even playing with the toggle at the end of the boat. And yet, people I work with say they have never seen seals in 'real life'. I have been followed by a whale, paddled alongside a swimming mink, seen basking sharks, sun fish, turtles, dolphins and porpoises from my boat, watched skuas in aerial combat with gannets just metres from my boat, watched an otter swim past with a huge lobster in its mouth, and been camped by my sea kayak when a sea eagle has tried to attack a Canadian Goose, just ten metres from where I sat. Sea kayaking seems to let you be 'in' the environment, in a way which nothing else I have ever done does.

Number 2. It allows you to escape modern civilisation. A sea kayak allows you to carry several weeks' worth of food, meaning you can stay out camping for a long time without too much reliance on civilisation. In fact that is what attracted me to it in the first place. I have always loved backpacking, but there is only so much food that a 5'3 girl can carry along with all camping gear, in a 75 litre rucksack. A sea kayak has carrying capacities of around 150 litres - that means a lot of days' food, a bit more comfort and a lot more red wine than can be carried on your back. I love 'trips' - packing my boat with everything I need for a few days to a few weeks, just living out of my boat, camping somewhere different every night, and that feeling of really travelling through an ever-changing landscape.

Number 3. It has made me realise we live on island. Sounds stupid I know, but I had just never really thought about the UK in this way. Now when I look at a map, I first see the coastline, not the land. The UK is an amazing sea kayaking country. Our islands stretch from the Channel Islands, significantly closer to France than the rest of mainland UK, to the Shetland Islands, with more affinity to Norway than the rest of the UK. We have coastline that sea kayakers from all around the world come to paddle, and they come regularly, many making several visits a year to some of our most famous coastal paddling regions, such as the coastline of Anglesey. So, with this world-renowned coast only two and a half hours drive from Stoke-on-Trent, suddenly it doesn't seem like such a stupid thing to take up sea kayaking living in a land-locked county, when I have now met many passionate sea kayakers who live in land-locked countries!

Number 4. It has an amazing international community. I have always been struck by the different "worlds" out there, whether that is the golfing world, the sailing world, the diving world or any other activity, each seems to have its own community. The sea kayaking community is a small one, but it is a close knit and very international one. One thing that seems quite distinctive about the sea kayaking 'world' are the regular symposia held in interesting coastal locations - generally weekend long gatherings of sea kayakers - days on the water, and evenings in the bar. These symposia often attract people from all over the world, and in particular, people who operate their own sea kayaking companies in other parts of the world will attend symposia in different countries. I now know that if I post on Facebook for recommendations of a sea kayaking outfitter in a part of the word I am travelling to for work, I'll inevitably get some recommendations for people who frequent the same paddling spots in Wales that I do on a regular basis, and a connection is already made. Sea kayakers the world over also seem very keen to show visitors their 'patch'.

Number 5. It provides great access. The sea has much better access laws than England and Wales. As a river paddler in England and Wales there is terrible and very restricted legal access to rivers. In contrast the sea around the UK, and land below the mean high water mark, is owned by the Crown, this means we have the right of access to these areas, which gives us a lot more paddling area than those restricting themselves to freshwater paddling. A sea kayak can also get you places along the coastline where almost nothing else can, allowing you to get into all those nooks and crannies that other boats can't get into. In some parts of the country, this can include huge caves, and arches, and subterranean passages that go through entire headlands.

Number 6. You're always learning. The sea always has something new to teach you. Sea kayaking requires you to be able to understand tides, and what the combined effects of wind, tide, swell and land will be on the state of the sea, and whether you want to be there. Anglesey provides such exceptional paddling, because of the tide races - areas where the tide is accelerated around headlands or shallows, creating conditions at particular states of tide, wind and swell that can either be great fun, or areas that you really need to avoid. Understanding and predicting this is a key aspect of paddling, and for me, I'd be honest and say that it is still throwing up surprises that I can learn from. I've made sure I've had a lot of coaching, and I've spent a lot of time paddling with people more experienced than myself, in order to gain this understanding, and be able to take other people out to learn from and enjoy this environment. If you want to start sea kayaking, make sure you take the time to learn from experienced people.

So, in summary. Sea kayaking has a reputation as being a boring 'beardy' sport. But I love the diversity of sea kayaking, it can be anything to anyone. It can be a calm paddle along some beautiful coastline, an extension to a day at the beach. It can be a paddle specifically to see wildlife, such as a known area for seals. It can be a weekend's wild camping expedition with friends, with a fire on the beach eating fresh fish caught from the kayak. It can be surfing at high speed down waves in a tide race far from land waves towering above your head, or surfing waves at a beach. It can be a months-long expedition carrying all of your food and camping equipment, taking you around entire islands or even countries, journeying to a new place every day. It can be an open crossing, over 12 hours paddling from the UK to Ireland for example. It can be anything else you want it to be. It can be as calm as you want or as adrenaline-fuelled as you want. But behind it all lies a need for an understanding of the sea and the ability to judge what conditions the sea will give you. I have seen amazing things, paddled beautiful areas, I have laughed, I have been in awe at my surroundings, and I have been scared. It is a sport, but at the heart of it is the element, the sea. And it is the sea which is the master, and the sea that will control what you do on any day. We must learn about the sea, try to predict how tide, wind, and the shape of the coastline and sea bed, will affect the sea at any particular time, and then how it will affect us and our boats.

Sea kayaking, like any sport, is good for fitness but it also provides me with much more than this, providing much more connection with the natural world than anything else I've ever done. I'm looking forward to exploring many other parts of the world by sea, and those same spots I return to every week, where the coastline and sea state is always slightly different, and there is always something new to see. And as for that carbon footprint, well there is a very good train connection from Crewe to Anglesey, and although there isn't yet a carriage for transporting sea kayaks, by storing or borrowing a boat on Anglesey, and getting someone to pick you up, then it's almost possible to live in Stoke and sea kayak without that environmental guilt!

42. One Day That Changed My Life

Ken Rushton

Ken Rushton is a much-respected and honoured member of the sports community in North Staffordshire and beyond. Ken continues to contribute a huge amount to the local running scene, not least as the race director of the iconic Potters 'Arf half marathon, held on the second Sunday in June each year.

1982. Overweight and unfit, my wife Sue and myself decided to go and watch the first Potteries Marathon which passed through Baddeley Green at mile 23 before finishing at Trubshaw Cross.

Something must have stirred in me to take some action. I knew a neighbour did some running to keep fit for rugby, so tagging along with him puffing and panting I couldn't even manage a mile. The next step of good fortune was finding a group of runners who used to train twice a week in Milton. I was quickly made welcome and after some training decided to take part in my first race at the end of 1982: the Madeley Half Marathon. Finishing in a respectable 1hr-37mins the bug had bitten me. Fast forward one year and I was on the start line for the 1983 Potts Marathon and four and a bit hours later I had done it.

A few things happened in the next couple of years: a 10k was to be organised in Milton and volunteers were being sought, this was the start of my organising career. Also I was introduced to the long run on a Sunday from the Michelin Athletic Club where runners from all clubs in the area trained together.

Last but not least in the list of people who have influenced my life, I was introduced to the great George Kay who explained the concept of North Staffs Road Runners to me, I was hooked, "how can I join?" I asked George, application form produced I was a member, not knowing 11 years later I would become Chairman of NSRRA a position I still hold today.

Training continued and I was always picking the brains of other runners, Mick Thacker, Norman Deakin and Don Shelley. My times continued to fall but I also discovered cross country which I quickly found I had a real affinity with. From 1984 until 1999 I only missed one North Staffs Cross Country Fixture, first of all with Newcastle AC, then one season with PMAC and finishing with Trentham RC.

Alongside my running career my organising continued, the Milton 10k achieving national acclaim in 1989 as it hosted the AAAs 10k Championship with an amazing field assembling. Course records of 28 minutes for the Men and 31 Minutes for the Ladies and the 100th runner clocking 35mins-10secs.

In 1990 the Milton organising team were asked to take over the running of the Alsager 5. This race is still successful today with over 1000 runners turning up in Alsager in February every year.

1995 was another turning point in my running life as I became a veteran and a group of us who trained together decided to join Trentham to see what we could achieve as veterans. For a number of years we were undefeated as a team and also taking many individual awards but the pinnacle was yet to be reached. In 1999 the British Veterans Marathon Championships were to be held in Wolverhampton and with months of training together the hard work we had put in saw us become British Marathon Champions and I had a Gold Medal. Wow I thought, what a journey, but in 2000 we decided to defend our Championship in the Isle of Man where the British Veteran Marathon Championships were to be held. The race date was August and my 45th birthday was the month before so I had two goals to aim at, those goals were achieved as we were successful in defending our Championship and I was over the moon to win an individual silver medal in my age category.

Sadly in 2005 I had to retire from running with a serious knee injury, luckily I still had the organising side to keep me involved. So where can I be found today? Well organising the Potters Arf and still looking after Alsager, still Chairman of North Staffs Road Runners and the North Staffs Cross Country League.

I was proud to receive the Tom Brennan award for Services to Sport in 2014 but as proud as I was to receive this award I have to pay tribute to the organising team around me and last but not least I must thank my wife Sue who has been my rock at my side throughout the whole of my running career both in competing and organising.

Thank you Sue.

43. Portrait of an Artist as a Working Man (extract)

Steve Shaw and Dave Proudlove

2016 saw a fascinating exhibition at the wonderful Airspace Gallery in Hanley, Stoke-on-Trent. Called 'Fools Rush In', it was a thought-provoking show by Leigh Clarke on the shallowness of celebrity and of celebrity autobiographies. As a counterpoint, six local writers were commissioned to ghost-write autobiographies of six local people (one from each of the six towns of Stoke-on-Trent) who had their own much richer life stories to tell.

Burslem's real-life hero was Steve Shaw the potter and artist, and his life-story was ghosted by Dave Proudlove. It is a privilege to be able to reproduce here an extract from 'Portrait of an Artist as a Working Man', where Steve talks about Stoke City FC as one of his sources of inspiration. Many thanks to Leigh Clarke, Glen Stoker of Airspace, Dave Proudlove and (not least) Steve Shaw for permission to publish this extract here. And we're doubly grateful to Steve for allowing us to feature some of his art alongside his story.

I will never forget my first match: a big European game under the lights as Dutch giants Ajax came to town. I wasn't really there for the football. Although I was just nine years old, I was there for the atmosphere, the experience: the noise, the smells, the kinship, the camaraderie.

People talk about culture, and this was real working class culture. And what a game to have marked down as my first. Although I wasn't there for the football, it seems ironic now that my Victoria Ground debut saw Stoke City take on a team of footballing artists. It is also ironic that for all the skills and flair on show, it was that force of nature from the Meir Denis Smith that scored for the Potters.

Denis Smith – painting by Steve Shaw, reproduced with permission of the artist

But footballing artistry was not exclusively foreign those days. The great Tony Waddington described football as "the working man's ballet", and brought a number of footballing artists to the Victoria Ground. For me, the greatest of all was Alan Hudson, who swapped the bright lights of London's Kings Road for the Six Towns. Hudson was a magician, and he even made simple warm up exercises in training look like a work of art. I once remember seeing him and couldn't understand why everyone wasn't banging on the window. I wasn't either, but inside I was screaming, "LOOK! IT'S ALAN HUDSON! LOOK! LOOK!"

It's been said that you should never meet your heroes, but I have been lucky enough to meet Alan, and not only that, I did a painting of him in his prime and he liked it. He did have a few things to say about it, which was a bit of an experience to say the least. He approached me in a bit of a haze, his eyes glazed, and told me I got him right, but that in the painting, he should have been wearing a granddad shirt ("I always wore granddad shirts"), which is interesting. Of all the photographs I pored over Hudson from his 1970s heyday, I never saw one of him in a granddad shirt. But Alan Hudson liked my painting, and that'll do for me.

'That' painting – Alan Hudson by Steve Shaw, reproduced with permission of the artist

44. The Match

Ilenia Sims

This is a lovely piece of creative writing from Ilenia. Alongside her writing skills, she's not a bad cricket player either, currently competing for Meakins Cricket Club women's team (with season's best of 6 for 10, and 110 not out), and for Staffordshire County Cricket Club in the U15 girls, U17 girls and the women's team. Her ambition is to play for England.

As she watched her brothers, cousins, father, uncles all play a game of cricket, her whole body was crippled with jealousy. "Girls don't play sports" her mother has declared to her. "Girls learn to cook, clean and care for families.". Yet, as much as she loved to cook, clean and care for people, just like mother had told her, she couldn't help the urge to try the game all the men in her family played. Cricket. All of the energy and emotions pouring out of the men, the quirky actions, the funky shots. She loved it from day one.

Every Saturday morning after coming home from the mosque, she would watch in awe as the men played their weekly game of cricket for fun on the acres of land behind their house and she would imagine she was there, joining in the dramatics, politics and friendships being created from this one game. While her sisters were playing with dolls, her mum and aunties were cooking and cleaning, she was sat at her bedroom window, gawping at the game.

Weeks went by, months went by, years went by and her connection with the sport never faded. Every Saturday she would always watch the game without fail, without missing one single second. It was an instant passion.

As time continued to fly by, it wasn't long until her 18th birthday and she had a massive party in her mansion of a house. It was a family party and all of her brothers, cousins, father and uncles were outside playing a game of cricket since they had no interest to be inside. A rush of energy came through her and she sprinted up to her room, took off her beautiful dress, which she chose to look like the women in the mosque, and chucked the first pair of trackies and sports top that came out of her wardrobe. This was her chance. As she leapt down the stairs, her mum shouted "Jaz, come back, what are you doing?", but her passion drove her outside like a chauffeur driving a VIP.

As she arrived by the umpire (who at this moment in time was her grandpa) she politely asked "Can I have a go?". Her grandpa was a lovely sympathetic man so he said in his sweet tone of voice "Of course Jaz, just keep your arm straight." "I know" blurted Jaz.

As she stormed in off a seven-pace run up, the men were all huffing and puffing that she was going to ruin the game, they didn't say it but it was in the atmosphere. As she gathered in her action, people's reactions began to change. As her front arm came up and her bowling arm fizzed over, there was a moment of wonder and speechlessness. The ball travelled bearing left and right constantly. It hit the deck and crashed into the stumps of her cousin. There was silence for a moment then bursts of cheers came in. This was the beginning and her chance.

Photos courtesy Laura Malkin Photography

45. Recollections of Stoke Speedway

Pat Sinclair

Speedway doesn't feature on our list of sports (those which get you fitter through exercise) but Pat's beautifully written piece really captures the community spirit and sense of well-being which comes through participating in any sport, even as a spectator. If you've ever been to Speedway then you'll find this story wonderfully evocative. And the poems are perfect too...

I was introduced to Speedway by my stepfather who took me and my Mum to the first meeting at Sun Street, Hanley in 1960. We were hooked immediately and went to every match which was usually held on a Saturday night. We were not alone. Thousands of supporters joined us and we soon became like one big family. Speedway, for all its noise and dirt, was very popular with all ages.

We used to stand in the same place every week, near to the tapes, so it wasn't long before we got to know the other supporters round about. Stoke's riders also became like family members: most of them lived locally and were more than happy to chat to the fans who often went round to the pits to see their favourites. The atmosphere during the races was electric. It was always a sad day when the current season ended and we couldn't wait for the new season to start. One year, they even had a match on Boxing Day. Luckily, there was no snow but it was bitterly cold. However, lots of supporters braved the weather to cheer on The Potters.

The promoters also arranged Speedway Balls at The Crystal in Newcastle and most of the riders attended - to the delight of the many fans. Well-known celebrities would often attend the meetings to present a cup to the most successful rider. That too was a highlight for we fans. One highlight for my Mum was when she was asked to present a cup to the winning rider and he took her round the track on his speedway bike. She was in heaven, particularly as she had a soft spot for the rider in question!

My Mum and I also wrote poems about Stoke Speedway which were printed in the programmes. These poems, by my mother Brenda, are on the following two pages. One of the poems mentions looking forward to the next season, but unfortunately, it all came to an end in 1963 when the owners of Sun Street Stadium put it up for sale. Speedway started up again at Loomer Road, Chesterton a few years later but it was never the same.

Ah well, all good things have to come to an end I suppose. We had three very happy, enjoyable years from 1960 to 1963, thanks to The Potters Speedway Team and the loyal supporters. Even now, when a motorbike goes past and gives off that distinctive smell from the exhaust - a mixture of alcohol and petrol, I'm transported back to Sun Street.

Oh to be in Hanley
Now that Speedway's back
And whoever comes to Sun Street
Sees the old familiar track;
When the tapes go up and the engines roar,
That's the sound the crowd adore
And the Potters' team each takes a bow
In Hanley-now!

ODE TO STOKE SPEEDWAY

Alas! This is the final meeting
And now the season ends,
And what will we do each Saturday
When we leave our Speedway friends?
We'll miss the roar of the engines,
The noise, the grit, the spills,
The wonderful smell of the exhausts,
The shouts, the mud, the thrills.
We've enjoyed every minute of the meetings,
And admired Stoke riders' skill
We wish them luck next season,
In fact, we always will.
So, till next season commences
We'll patiently wait once more
For the wonderful sound of the engines-
The good old "POTTERS" roar!

ALL THE VERY BEST TO EVERYONE CONNECTED WITH STOKE SPEEDWAY
Frank, Brenda and Pat.

46. My Sporting Story: Squash

Angela Smith

Angela Smith is a former world champion squash player, winning the 1979 Women's World Team Squash Championships, and she was one of the world's highest ranked players throughout the 1980's. Playing squash has allowed her to travel the world and she has been involved in numerous initiatives internationally to develop the sport. She is currently chair of Stoke City Supporters Council, a director of the Sir Stanley Matthews Coaching Foundation, and chairs the European City of Sport Local Organising Committee.

When I cast my mind back to how I started in the sport, luck played a part. I played tennis at Hanley Park with friends and this particular summer, it was a pretty dull wet affair. As a result, most of our games and practise were called off. My mum had seen a couple of lines in the Evening Sentinel newspaper which stated that three squash courts had been built at Northwood Stadium and mentioned it in passing, so myself and Tony Gordon decided to go along and take a look on one of the days when rain stopped play.

To be honest, we had no idea what squash entailed, other than it was played in a room which was like a box with a door and that was it. It is fair to say that my and Tony's first entry into the sport was low key, we didn't even know that you had to get the ball warm in order for it to bounce! Luckily (again) the manager gave us a couple of rackets and a swift recap of a few simple rules and our love affair with squash began. We booked the court for the following week in case it rained, it did and we became hooked on the sport.

The great thing about squash is that you can get an enormous amount of exercise in a short amount of time and you don't need to worry about the weather. You can always find players of all standards at local clubs due to the league systems where you can play competitively if you wish. Squash appealed to me because of the amount of exercise I got quickly, the way I could hit the ball to get rid of any frustration and aggression that I had and the social aspect was good too.

I was "sporty", playing tennis and hockey for the school and I was okay at other ball games and athletics, but I was pretty rubbish at gymnastics and dance so I do understand why some people don't like sport at all. The fact is that when we get to around 15, life changes and we have to consider serious study or working! Squash will give you a workout in a short space of time as you move into adulthood and if you are already in adult life it will help you exercise some muscles that you may have forgotten exist! After around six months, I found that playing squash was affecting my tennis and vice versa and I decided that I enjoyed squash much more than tennis, funnily enough Tony felt the same and we both continued with squash.

I have no doubt that winning a tournament early on in my career helped spur me on and I worked very hard to get to the top of the ladder. I also trained to get qualifications in case I was unsuccessful or sustained an injury which would prevent me from playing. I would say that is really important as no matter how good you are, age always wins in the end!

I have met famous people that I would never have dreamed of. Travelled the world and made lifelong friends through squash - all thanks to my mum mentioning a small article in the local paper. More importantly, I have been fit and healthy and enjoyed my life locally as a result of hitting a little black ball in a box with a door. I recommend taking up a sport to everyone, the benefits physically and emotionally are in my opinion underestimated.

47. The Chirp

Jeremy Snape

Thanks to Stoke-on-Trent born former England cricketer Jeremy Snape, who contributed this great little story about a chirp (best described as banter on the cricket pitch).

Everyone loves a chirping story in cricket and most are obscene but this one is shareable. In the late 90's I was playing for Northants against the touring West Indians – think Lara, Walsh, and Ambrose. I had the usual nerves walking out to bat against fast bowlers but my first challenge was to navigate their leg spinner Dhanraj.

With numerous legends crowded around the bat I faced a few balls and played and missed at most. Googlies, top spinners and leg spinners kept me guessing and as the pressure built, so did the chirping. I remember thinking that I'd rather face Courtney Walsh than have this humiliation so resorted to my last option – a slog over extra cover.

As I swung, head up through the line of the next spinning ball, I snicked it with a faint edge. Of course there was huge excitement in the West Indies camp with Brian Lara at slip leading the way – the difference was that I had rocked onto my front foot to walk and then in a moment of indecision, rocked back to stay my ground. This moment was met by a cacophony of jeers and abusive comments amounting to 'you can't be serious mate'.

I was taking the flack when the hammer blow arrived, and it was not the fact that Courtney Walsh was instructed to warm up, it was Jimmy Adams walking from his nearby position at short leg, lifting up his fielding helmet and stating in a deep but almost saintly voice "may the Lord have mercy on you". I have to say my guilt level went through the roof with this sinful act and it remains the most memorable chirp of my career.

Admiral

48. It Seemed a Good Idea at the Time...

David Steele

Monday 16th May 2011
Entries close tomorrow. Can I find the courage to post my form off? Or, with two of my mates already entered, can I find the courage not to?

The Anfield '100' is the oldest cycle race in the country, and possibly in the world. Promoted each year on the roads of Cheshire and Shropshire it was first held in 1889. At my age will I have any more opportunities? I gather my resolve, complete the entry form, pop it in an envelope with a cheque for £10 and drop it into the post box at the end of the road.

Tuesday 24th May 2011
My start sheet arrives. I scan down the list of riders. I'm there...*David Steele, Lyme Racing Club, Age 71, Start time 6.13am.* Displayed on the front cover is a grainy photograph of a Ben Orrell, on the start line of the 1930 event. He wears what looks like a casual jacket, while the timekeeper is smartly dressed with collar and tie. I recall my father clad in similar attire when tending to our front garden. Times have changed.

Apprehensively I check that John and Kenny's names are on the list. They are. John is off 15 minutes behind me at 6.28am and Kenny at 7.08am. So they have kept their word and both entered, which in some ways is a relief. At least now we shall be able to share accounts of our sufferings after the event.

Spring Bank Holiday Monday 30th May 2011

At 3.45am the alarm clock jolts me out of my peace. I ease myself out of bed, part the curtains and survey the heavens. Even in the limited light of early dawn the clouds look threatening. A quick glance at the thermometer shows 43F, uncomfortably cold for the time of year. Everything had been prepared the previous evening. A bowl of porridge followed by toast and a mug of tea soon disappear. A bag containing spare clothes and towel, together with bananas, squeegee packs of energy-gel to carry in my racing vest pockets and bottles of Lucozade were placed by the front door so my vital requirements wouldn't be left behind.

John has promised to collect me at 4.45am for the drive out to Shawbury. My cat's ears twitch as she detects the crunching of grit on the driveway. I knew John wouldn't let me down as he has prepared well for the event and this could be his moment of glory. We make good time to the race H.Q. but the blobs of rain on the windscreen become larger and closer, but fail to prepare us for what lies ahead.

We step out of the warmth of John's plush vehicle, gather our bikes from the rear and enter the H.Q. The place is awash with activity. I sign the declaration form, and a pretty lady gives me my 13 race number. Someone mentions that riders off number 13 are allowed to pin their number on upside down. I'd never heard of that before so I don't bother. A quick cup of tea, an even quicker visit to the toilet, then I shake hands with John and Kenny, wish them good luck, and set off on the three mile ride to the start.

In the pouring rain it seems a long three miles. But eventually I see a cluster of people in a lay-by. A few of them are riders due off before me, together with the timekeeper, other officials of the Anfield Bicycle Club and a gentleman holding a large black umbrella dutifully sheltering each rider as he or she is held up on the start line. Rider number 12 is sent on his way. The timekeeper studies his watch. I 'scoot' to the start-line where a gentleman grips my bike to hold me upright. I 'click' my racing shoe cleats into the pedals. *One* *minute…thirty seconds… fifteen seconds…ten seconds…five seconds…*I start my computer… *four…three…two…one… go…best of luck.* And I'm off.

The route is quite straightforward. A 32 mile stretch to Whitchurch roundabout and return to Shawbury. Then four 17 mile circuits through Crudgington and Hodnet, back to Shawbury to complete the 100 miles. I reach the turn at Whitchurch and glance at my watch. John started 15 minutes after me, so if I ride back for 7 minutes and 30 seconds before we 'cross' we shall be level on race time. At precisely that time John rides past going in the opposite direction. He shouts across to me, he looks good, appears cheerful and more worryingly, sounds confident. John is a successful businessman and devoted husband, father and grandfather. To catch me in a time trial is perhaps his last remaining ambition. He will have prepared beforehand what to shout when he catches me. And it looks as if the opportunity might have arrived.

The rain and cold continue. I reach Shawbury, and, managing to resist the lure of the H.Q., turn left, to start the first of the four laps. My clothes are now becoming sodden, the cold creeping into my bones. I fumble around in one of my vest pockets, and somehow, with fingers resembling icicles, manage to grasp a banana, strip off the skin with my teeth and quickly swallow the contents before they break off and provide a meal for hungry ravens. Then follows an energy-gel rinsed down with gulps of Lucozade. Food provides calories. Calories provide warmth. I continue in slightly better spirits and eventually complete the first lap.

I repeat the food and drink regime on my second lap, but the rain continues and the roads are becoming flooded. And I feel that my efforts to keep warm are slowly being eroded.
The third of the 17 mile laps has arrived. Within a few miles I begin to feel that my entire being is succumbing to the cold. My mind is becoming rather disorientated and I begin to fear the onset of hypothermia. I wonder whether I could stop at one of the isolated farmhouses and ask if the owner would offer warmth. Then I recall that a race marshal is

situated at the junction at Crudgington just a mile or so further down the road. I reach him and ask if he could somehow take a flimsy lightweight jacket from one of my vest pockets. My clothes are clinging together, but he manages to extract it in one piece. He opens it out, threads my shaking arms through the sleeves, and zips it closed, and helps me back on my bike. I thank him, but not as warmly as I should. My legs still feel quite strong and in a few miles I detect some semblance of warmth. The jacket has now obscured my race number, I must shout it out to any marshal that I see.

My fourth and final lap has arrived. It gives comfort to know that each yard that I cover is for the last time. The rain still falls, the floods are deeper and more frequent, but neither John nor Kenny have caught me and without mechanical problems I feel more confident that I can finish. Approaching Shawbury I see the chequered flag in the distance. I shout my number out to the timekeeper and press the 'stop' button on my computer. I wipe away the raindrops, and it indicates 101 miles. Obviously I must not have calibrated it quite correctly beforehand.

Just a few hundred yards and I am back in the warmth of the H.Q. And guess who meet me at the doorway? John and Kenny had both failed to finish, calling it a day, numb with cold at the end of the first lap. They congratulate me, help me to a chair, where John kindly wraps a woollen shawl round me and Kenny fetches cups of hot sweet tea.

We stay and watch the prize presentation. The winner, Andy Bason had covered the hundred miles in 3 hours, 41 minutes, 7 seconds and there is generous applause as he receives the £200 prize. No awards for me, I have to be content with the knowledge that I managed to finish when so many others had failed.

But then a few days later a lovely surprise. I receive a letter in the post enclosing the result brochure and a cheque for £30 for being the faster rider in the event for riders over 70 years of age. I'm sure John and Kenny will be absolutely delighted when I let them know!

49. My Sporting Story: Time for a Change

Liz Tideswell

I moved to Stoke-on-Trent in 2009 (I married a local) and found that life in my new home was enjoyable but not really conducive to my health and wellbeing. I was much more sedentary than I'd been whilst living in London, doing very little exercise and gaining weight. I couldn't even run for a bus and the ten minute walk from my house to the shops became an ever growing challenge. By November 2010 I knew it was ***time for a change***... Working on the mantra of eat less, exercise more, I changed my diet, switched to a smaller dinner plate and started using the exercise bike that had been gathering dust in my garage.

It worked!

Over the first three months, I lost the weight I'd put on and more besides. I started to feel better and healthier. But a few months into my fitness and weight loss journey, I decided I needed another goal. After some internet searching, I came across the *Couch to 5k* programme and almost immediately set out for my first run along the canal towpath. Just one minute of running felt like a marathon but after a few weeks, I could run for 10 minutes and then 15 minutes and then 20 and then 30 minutes of running without stopping. I signed up for the Race for Life at Trentham Gardens, wanting to prove to myself that I really was going from couch to 5k.

I was inspired!

About that time, from my kitchen window overlooking the canal, I noticed groups of women running by on Tuesday and Thursday evenings, mostly wearing pink and looking like running was fun. They were smiling and chatting and, most importantly, they looked like real people and not elite athletes. I'd never considered joining a running club - I wasn't a runner - but these women inspired me to give it a try. By the wonders of the Internet again, I discovered that they were the Potters Trotters - a ladies only running club at that time based at Northwood Stadium but now meeting at Staffordshire University's Leek Road campus. I sent an email, was invited along and nervously joined them for my first run. I think I managed about three miles and still remember being excited that I hadn't needed to stop.

I was hooked!

Running twice a week with the pink ladies became a habit and my health and wellbeing continued to improve. Every week, with every conversation, I heard inspiring stories of women just like me who had done the extraordinary - completing marathons, half marathons and 10k races, transforming their outlook on life and getting out and about in their city. I dipped my toe in the water of racing and completed my first 10k, dressed as a Christmas Pudding.

I felt at home!

Running also helped me to almost get my bearings in my new home, following the canal towpath out to Westport Lake, running along the cycle way to Norton, heading out to Trentham Gardens and always getting confused by the different routes to Newcastle. I learnt about the hills and my new running friends told me about the challenge of the Potters 'Arf, although it was a while before I braved Anchor Road and Milton Road.

I just kept running!

Hanley parkrun became a weekly habit and I'm still there most weekends as a runner or core volunteer. I signed up for the Stafford Half Marathon, then the Potters 'Arf and even had a go at cross country! My club mates helped with training plans and ran with me in the dark days of winter, gently persuading me that a marathon was well within my capabilities. In April 2013 in Manchester, they stood on the finish line and cheered me on as I completed my first marathon and then selected me to represent them at the London Marathon in 2014. The support and inspiration that started with the Potters Trotters eventually took me all the way across Staffordshire, as in March 2016, I completed the 41 miles of the Millennium Way from Newport to Burton upon Trent.

I'll keep on running!

I'm not sure what comes next in my sporting story – there are many challenges out there to tempt me – but hopefully I'll be able to keep on running and encouraging other people to run too. If I can, you can. It's time for a change.

50. A Day in the Life of a Ball

David Tierney

Another imaginative and creative contribution from a St Joseph's College pupil – this one by David has a great punchline!

Hello, sporty people
I am a newly-bought ball
I want to find out which ball I am
For I don't know yet at all!

I have a friend – a football
He is rather shy
For when he meets a human
He's always kicked sky-high!

Then there is the volleyball
Always slapped and hit
I don't fancy that at all
I don't, not a bit!

I know a little tennis ball
Who also is hit over a net
They're always being hit with a racket
That must hurt, I bet!

The rugby ball as you know of course
Is jostled, shoved and pounded
I'm glad I'm not one of them
I'm spherical, not rounded (oval rounded)

So, what ball am I?
I think I'm going to find out!
The human is picking me up and throwing
And I'm caught in an animal's slobbery mouth!

Photo courtesy St Joseph's College

51. Road to Africa

Matthew Wilcock

Matthew got to know Middleport Pottery in Stoke-on-Trent very well as a competitor and ultimately the winner in the BBC's 2015 Great Pottery Throwdown. As well as being a very skilled potter, he's also got form as a cyclist...

My name is Matthew and on the 10th of July 2015, after little planning and hardly any organisation, I began the solo cycle from Orkney to Africa. I first bought a bike for the same reason every other post-graduate in their early twenties does: to go on epic pub crawls with their mates in the summer - we've still not got round to this. It was beautiful: a kind of rusty beige, but faded green in places where the sun hadn't quite got to. Costing me the princely sum of two pints, she only needed new tyres, tubes, brakes, chain, and everything else that moved. She was a Peugeot from the late 70s that had belonged to many previous pub crawlers. I felt as though I was part of the new generation, I was sure the adventures we would have together would be out of this world.

As the year went on, I soon decided the Peugeot desperately wanted to be turned into a single-speed or fixie. So, after stripping the entire frame, buying entirely new parts for everything and even a new paint job ("Rolls Royce Silver"), she was back on the road! The decision to transform my iron steed was mainly based on living in Preston, where it is flat and, obviously, I wanted to look cool because that was what all the hipsters rode.

It was that summer, on a campsite near Valencia, that I met Anthony. The second I saw him, I knew he was British and I knew he'd cycled the whole way. He had begun at the famous John O'Groats and was ending in Gibraltar. That evening we sat in the bar discussing, in detail, every part of his adventure to date. Anthony explained that he had just finished college and in September he was starting at Land Rover Jaguar: he would never again have that length of time to do what he wanted. I immediately agreed with this. I don't know how long I will be in education. Therefore, I am very fortunate to have long summers and should make the most of them. This might have been the moment I decided to cycle to Africa.

On my return from Spain, I went straight to the local bike shop and spent rather a lot more than I had spent on my first bike. I was moving to the Dales, so a fixie wouldn't be the most appropriate of bikes, especially not for Buttertubs, one of the roads the tour used. I soon felt like a pro on my shiny carbon push bike. I would be out training every day, wind, rain sleet - and this was October. The more I cycled, the more I became addicted to it. I was feeling stronger every day. Quicker, with every ride.

I understood why people loved it. It was just me on my own, no worries or concerns. I had the opportunity to think about things which mattered to me. As an artist it is very important to reflect on one's thoughts which can´t always be the easiest thing. Cycling had just given me the answer of how to do this. With the winter out of the way, I became conscious that the following summer I would be cycling to Africa. I started stepping up the miles and even thought about what I was eating. Occasionally, at work, whilst opening emails, I'd have a quick glance at a map of France or Spain, this was the planning stage.

In the spring of that year, I was lucky enough to be introduced to nine amazing people and had the chance to participate in what was probably going to be the opportunity of a lifetime. Filming "The Great Pottery Throw Down" didn't come without its consequences though. With a huge cutback to my cycling and an increased diet, of which was just chocolate and crisps, training was not going well. Also, I think the psychological effect of having to cycle to Africa was playing with my mind slightly.

However, with about four weeks to go, filming was done. I treated myself to some panniers, a lightweight tent, sleeping bag and lots of really cool gadgets I was sure I would need for my trip through Europe. I told my parents of my plan, or lack of one, asked a friend to drive me up to John O'Groats and that was it.

Photo reproduced with permission. Copyright B.P.M. Harris

I hadn’t intended Orkney to be the start point however, after the eight hour drive up I thought it would be a kind of thank you to my friend if we did a bit of touring around. So we got the ferry over, cycled, and I cooked us a lovely tea. This was more for me really, as I would only have hot food once on my trip. This was to save weight on carrying a stove.

Orkney was gorgeous. Because it was summer it didn't really go dark in the evening, it just stayed that lovely dusk kind of grey with the orange harbour lights shimmering across the water. We both rose at 5am to get the first ferry back to the mainland, I wish I could say I had a restful night but that would be a lie. There was just so much to think about!

We were back to John O’Groats in good time and after the obligatory photo by the legendary signpost I was off. That first mile was the hardest mile of my life. I realised I’d never ridden a bike with panniers before, so balancing was a bit different. By the time I worked out how to ride this contraption, I was out of the car park and up the hill, at which point I had a quiet little cry to myself. Just the first of a few short emotional breakdowns, which are to be expected when doing stupid things such as this.

After I pulled myself together, I felt great. I was on my own, doing exactly what I had been thinking about for the previous year. What's more, it didn't feel difficult, it was almost as if my training was paying off. My cheery, light-hearted mood was soon damped with rain. As the hills became bigger and the rain heavier, I grew weaker. I had told myself to take regular breaks and not to push hard on the pedals. It seemed to be working but let's be honest: cycling any distance with about 20kgs on the back was going to be tiring.

Occasionally I would pass another tourer going the other way up the A9, just about to finish the end to end. We'd smile and wave, then exchange that look of mutual respect. I would grow to love that cheeky glance, it was a kind of high five mixed in with a pep talk, like we were in a special club. I would then think if only they knew I wasn't going to stop till Africa. Thinking about it, it's amazing how much can be communicated through eye contact and a smile.

I did 108 miles that first day and it felt like it! The first few days are always going to be the worst, every touring blog I'd ever read told me that. I'm not sure if it's what I was expecting though, it seemed very difficult and there didn't seem to be any immediate rewards.

With day one under my belt, I woke up feeling a lot better than I had imagined. Usually, the second day can be the worst, as you feel the pain from the first but you need to carry on, as your body adapts to this new routine. However, resting was not an option. With the weather almost as wet as the day before, I hastily stuffed everything into the panniers and cracked on. The long climb out of Inverness was not the easiest of climbs, it dragged on for a long time and confused me into thinking maybe my fitness was dropping. My spirits quickly perked up as I passed a sign saying I was at Slochd Summit, 1328ft. You know if there's a sign then you must be pretty high.

Long descents are fun! They're even more fun when you have the road to yourself. I soon got knocked back to reality with a puncture. I had hoped to last a bit longer than two days but these things happen. I was quite happy to repair it because I thought I need to get used to being independent, problem solving, fixing things that break and all that. I was less happy to receive my second puncture no more than 15 minutes after my first. Oh well, there was nothing I could do but repair it again and hope for the best.

I was riding a lot more confidently now I had discovered the pace that worked well for me. Not putting in any more power than was necessary and stopping regularly, either to eat or to look at the route. This worked well, at the end of the day, I was in no rush. I would later on begin to understand this more and more. You do things when you want and how you want, because, when you're on the road, it's just you that matters.

With day two complete in good time, there was chance to get a few beers and relax in the sun by my tent. The following day was a real test of my navigational skills: after Perth it was a case of zig-zagging my way through A and B roads, this was a sign of what was to come. My trip through Edinburgh was made considerably easier though as a beautiful medical student guided me along the cycle ways into the centre. I must have seemed incredibly confused and lost.

When I crossed the border to England, I felt a great sense of achievement. My first country done! All in all it wasn't too bad, all I had to do now was repeat that another seven times. What did make me feel better though wasn't the man playing bagpipes, but as I entered England, as if by magic, the rain stopped. From here on, the weather would be perfect.

I found it incredibly easy to ride through the north. The roads were quiet and they all seemed to go to where I wanted them to. I got to York for lunch on day five and I'm really glad my route took me straight through the centre. I knew York was a city with great culture, however, this was my first visit. It was wonderful to discover new and interesting places even in my own country.

The next day was my first test of problem-solving. Peterborough at rush hour and my chain snapped. How does a chain snap after 600 miles? I actually had every bike tool but a chain splitter. Thankfully, it wasn't quite the end of the working day and I managed to google a local bike shop. After explaining what I was doing they even drove out to take me back to their workshop. Such amazing people!

With my chain fixed and a printed out map of the country roads, steering me clear of the A14, I was on my way. That night, I was to camp just outside of Cambridge. Cycling through the centre, I had never seen a place so populated with bikes. For the first time, I felt like a tourist, stopping to take photos and marvel at centuries old, architectural masterpieces.

I usually have some kind of guilt about being a tourist. I don't like the fondling with maps and capturing every moment with my phone to then upload to social media, but this was the first time I wanted to explore the entire city. Sadly, I was on a time limit to get the ferry.

It was then on day seven I had the worst pain from cycling I'd ever come across. Approaching London, my knees began to ache badly, similar to what I had felt before on long rides. After London, the pain was close to unbearable. So much so that I took it in turns pedaling with different legs. Having read books since, I have learnt that this was probably tendinitis. Something that is common in endurance events. I told myself if tomorrow was the same, I would need a rest day and have to slow down the pace. The pain was almost over, as I rolled along the last five miles of England to my Dover campsite. Of course such an accomplishment could not be completed without a puncture.

Having crossed the English Channel, or "La Manche," I was now in Calais, granted, not the best introduction to France, but by no means as bad as the media leads us to believe. Because I had no phone service abroad, I was solely reliant on a map I had downloaded.

Some might say bad planning on my behalf. This meant no googling the nearest bike shop, or campsite and no ringing for help if things went wrong. I was now by myself.

This was the start of my real adventure. So, how better to start a real adventure than with a puncture on the main road through Calais? I rather enjoyed that first day of France, part of my family are French so I feel quite at home, cycling through the little villages. Somehow there is a sense that life moves at a different pace abroad. That evening I found a slightly strange campsite with what you might call 'traditional' French toilets. I listened to the rain gently fall onto my tent at night and it soothed me to sleep. I woke the next morning excited to get on the road. I had planned to stop at my cousin's house near Paris and I couldn't wait.

By now I felt I was a pretty experienced tourer. My knees had broken through that pain barrier, I knew my pace, my cadence, when to eat, when to drink and importantly when to rest. I didn't have to consciously think about that stuff every second, now spend my time pondering the important things and reflecting on life.

Once again, standing in the way of reflection time were punctures. That day I used the last of my repair patches, I now had none. I could not get another puncture. It was also a Sunday, this meant no bike shops.

After much careful cycling I soon arrived at the old home of Claud Monet, the famous French impressionist. Just five more kilometres and I would be at Katya's house. I have extremely fond memories of Les Metz Village. I spent most of my childhood holidays there, playing in a stream made famous by one of Monet's paintings.

I arrived, expecting some sort of welcome banner; they might have invited friends to congratulate me. Neither of this was true, in fact, they weren't even home. Eventually both cousin and boyfriend returned. Katya cooked me a large variety of carbs and Jean-Charles supplied me with beer. I was in heaven. I even had an actual bed to sleep in! I think, by this point it's fair to say I deserved a lie-in.

However, it wasn't difficult to find motivation to get up and organise myself, after all, I was about to hit 1000 miles. Before leaving I made sure to test every single type of chocolate and biscuity form of treat my cousin stocked, and as a primary school teacher, there were ample amounts. Also, of course, I could not pass the opportunity of making myself a coffee, the first one since John O'Groats. I really love coffee; therefore, it had been a hard week to function without.

The absolute priority for that day was to find a bike shop. I tried many shops that morning and eventually came to the conclusion that all bike shops close on a Monday, I presume so the owner can go cycling. Thankfully, by chance a group of cyclers flew past me, managing to talk to one of them I explained my problem and I was soon given an inner tube, almost as though I needn't have asked. He was probably a bike shop owner.

With a colossal weight lifted from my shoulders I continued along the perfectly straight roads which cut their way through the cereal fields of France. I found these relaxing as I didn't have to think about steering, just admire what was around me. As I approached 990 miles I began to look for a bar to reward myself. It was easy to see I was in the middle of nowhere and this was not going to be an option. Fate, on the other hands, had other plans. I was instead to spend my 999.8th mile – yes, you guessed it - repairing a puncture.

As I worked my way further south, things actually couldn't get much easier. I'd managed to find a rather quiet A road which would take me about 400 miles without having to put much thought into navigation; an absolute godsend after the South of England. I found a bike shop which resembled Aladdin's cave, so stocked up on inner tubes.

The weather by this point was perfect! A warm breeze and clear blue sky. Also I stopped worrying about a destination for the evenings as almost every town I passed had at least one campsite, so I could just cycle until the day was up and then just look for camping signs. This rather spontaneous way of touring led me to find one of the best sites I've ever stayed at. My tent was pitched next to a lake that had a sandy beach, with a bar on it, absolutely brilliant night.

The next day I continued with ease down through Bergerac. When I originally thought about the route through France, I had a rather romantic image in my head of myself, sitting outside a chateau, enjoying red wine amongst the vineyards, with a good selection of cheese in front of me. I might also have been wearing a beret. This image did not happen. Instead, I merely glanced towards the miles and miles of vines as I made my way through wine country and towards the Pyrenees.

This was the day I had been rather anxious about for quite some time. In fact, ever since I found out the Tour de France was to take the same route over the Pyrenees. I therefore hypothesised that it was not going to be an easy day. It didn't start well either, as I noticed that I had been robbed during the night by some French youths. Fair enough, it was only a power bank, but when you need it to charge a phone to access maps of Spain, it kind of becomes a lifeline. Fortunately, this issue was soon resolved by some early morning retail therapy.

As I pedalled on towards Spain the mountains began to grow around me, I was in awe as this was by far the most beautiful scenery I had witnessed on the trip. I stopped before the serious climbing, began to top up on carbs, sugar and liquids. Got myself psyched up and hit the road! I was extremely careful to pace myself when the road became steeper. I had regular breaks, which was not difficult at all, as this gave me a chance to admire the view. You know you're on a proper climb, when there is a sign every kilometre telling you what altitude you are, the gradient of the climb and how far from the top you are. These are great for reminding you of how little progress you're making, as well as how much more pain you are about to endure. I say that, and it's true: it was a demanding day, but there isn't one second of that ride I didn't enjoy. As I weaved my way closer to the top my surroundings became breath-taking. Not only could I see for miles all around, the only noise I heard was that of the cows and their huge steel bells. These would echo though the mountains creating some incredible sounds. The thing I loved the most though, had to be the hairpin corners of the road, this was my first introduction to real cycling roads and I couldn't get enough of them. A famous quote, "not everyone can play on the same pitch as their favourite footballer but you can ride on the same roads as your favourite cyclists." I was astonished to have that tiny insight into what the peloton go through on a tour. Agreed, at a completely different level, however, an experience to say the least. Having reached Arétte-Pierre-Saint-Martin, I thought I had earned myself an espresso at the ski station and savoured my last few moments on French soil before the final push over the top into Espagna.

The contrast between two days of cycling was incredible, I had only gone over a few mountains but suddenly the temperature shot up and the landscape became very barren. Everywhere I looked was this dusty, ochre coloured, dirt with the occasional twiggy bush. Once again, navigating was pretty easy. There's not much in the middle of Spain, so there isn't much reason to have a lot of roads.

There are bad points to this though. Firstly, if you do take a wrong turn, you're probably about 20km in the other direction before you realise. Secondly, you learn to get good at stocking up on water because once you leave a village that's it for another hour or two. Unless you find a graveyard, they always have taps.

After two days of cycling through the northern part of Spain I had my first wild camp. As per usual, I reached about 80 miles and started looking on the map for towns in the next

20 miles. Found one, got there, no campsite. This was a very exciting moment for me but also a scary and quite anxious one, too.

I wanted to wild camp on my trip because that was a tick box to an adventure. So, I decided simply to cycle till sunset and pitch up. This way I'd get extra miles in and no one would see my tent when I set up camp. By pure chance (and if you've been to central Spain, you'd understand) I reached a lovely forest and home for that night. I walked for 15 minutes down a sandy, over-grown, dirt track to make sure I was well out of the way of anyone. Then a car drove past, I put this down to pure chance. With a slight bit of adrenalin I cleared some space amongst some pine trees for my tent. It's strange isn't it, you feel safest paying to camp five metres from someone you've never met before. However, when you're 20 miles from the nearest town it suddenly becomes quite eerie.

After a nutritious meal of nuts, beer and tuna, I went straight to bed. Lying awake with my senses turned up to max, I heard the rustling outside my tent. At first I tried to ignore it telling myself it's just my imagination and it's probably just a rabbit. I knew it wasn't though; far too big. Gently unzipping my door, I plucked up the courage to glance out from my tent. I then saw five or more deer, no more than 30ft away. They didn't startle one bit and seemed just as interested in me as I was in them. I watched them for a short while as well as looking up to one of the brightest starry skies I've ever seen.

Something I have learnt from following cyclists on Twitter is that every athlete has their 'worst day'. Mine happened on day 21, it was about 42 degrees, and it pushed me to my limit both mentally and physically. The day before hadn't ended well as my face was blistered, my lips had split badly, and I had to pay £20 for a campsite.

So, after not sleeping because of the heat, I set off into the closest thing to a desert I had ever seen. It was actually quite beautiful. There was nothing around but the horizon and a straight road, not even any traffic. Everything went well until lunch when things started to heat up. The tortilla I bought had fermented and exploded in my pannier bag, which was now an oven. This wasn't a huge problem though, just a mess.

Following my siesta under the olive trees, I continued. It was now over 40 degrees and I was averaging more than a litre of water an hour, locals clearly realised I was insane as people driving past would wind down windows and offer water. There was no shade at this point and my phone, with all my maps and strava, had decided to give up. The only way I could cool it down was to hold it under a road sign, the only shade in sight. Unbelievably, this worked! However, as I was drinking more water than I could carry, and with few services it wasn't long until I became hugely dehydrated. I laugh at the thought of it now but I remember being angry at anyone for not planting a tree for shade. I just couldn't understand why there was no shade anywhere. It was like a really hard maths problem. I had to stop and have a little paddy by the side of the road. I was in a lot of pain. Emotional breakdown over, I forced myself onwards and it didn't take too long to find supplies.

Unfortunately, even though I bought enough supplies, I clearly hadn't learnt. This would be the last shop that day. As the mountains started the roads became incredibly difficult.

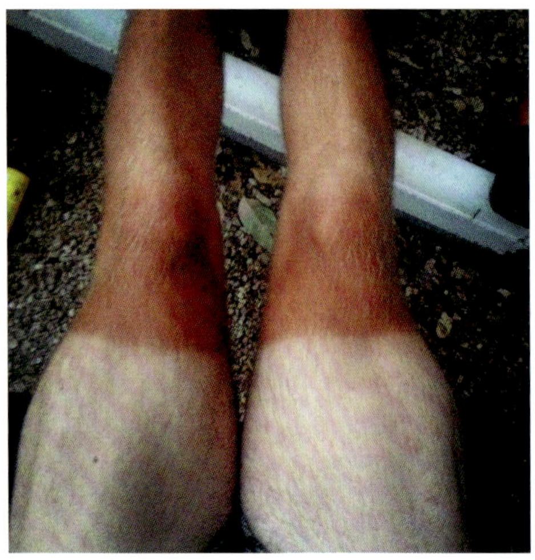

There was plenty of writing on the roads, a good sign they are used for the Vuelta (Spanish Tour de France), not what you want to see when you are unprepared. Again, finishing the last of my water I also ate the final piece of chocolate. I think I cried a little when I found a tap, it's like someone had placed it there just for me and I couldn't care less if it was drinkable or not. That night, I found a lovely campsite and pitched up next to a Belgian cyclist, also cycling across Spain but the opposite way to me. We both sat in a bar that night sharing stories of our tour and of course showing off each other's tan lines (mine won).

My final day of cycling was incredible. Winding my way down through the mountain roads, watching Gibraltar on the horizon growing larger. I'm not sure if I did spend the entire 60 miles descending but that's what it felt like. I soon arrived at the British border, which was a bit of an anti-climax.

I had expected police asking me where I had cycled from, and then telling their mates and everyone being amazed. Instead I cycled through customs, held my passport up to someone that didn't seem to care, and carried on across the runway (to get to Gib you need to cross the runway).

I choose to treat myself to a hostel that night, having earned it, then went to explore. I made a stop at Morrison's and satisfied some cravings, steak and ale pie obviously and of course bought some shower gel as I had run out and didn't smell great. The next morning I rose early to get the ferry to Africa, just a short ride along the cost, buy a ticket, job done. Not that easy. If you've wondered what it's like cycling on a motorway for 10 miles, take it from me: absolutely terrifying!

Arriving at the terminal wasn't much better either. I've never experienced so much chaos. The Arabs have a saying: "the louder you shout the more you get". Every single person in that building seemed to agree with this. There is so much I could say about the six stressful hours I spent in that building, however, I hope this sums it up; I bought a ticket for what turned out to be freight, I ended up (eventually) as a foot passenger on a different company's ferry, (apparently you get the first one you see), I think I then got a visa, then I disembarked as a vehicle because they didn't quite know what to make of my bike. To this day I am still baffled as to how I got across that sea.

If anyone ever wants to know what it feels like to be a professional cyclist: ride a bike in Morocco. For the 60km from the port to Tangier the roads were full of people clapping, cheering and occasionally holding out their hands for high-fives. It's like everyone knew that I had just cycled for more than 3 weeks solid to get there. I think the reality is they're just not used to seeing cyclists and probably thought I was crazy. Upon arriving at my hostel in the old city walls, I was greeted by travelers from across the world. This was exactly what I had imagined, a huge group of adventurists, each with their own unique story, tales of where they had been and advice on what to do. It was incredible to meet people so like-minded, you instantly became friends. That evening we sat on top of the hostel roof, right in the centre of the medina. We had beer, a BBQ and a guitar. I feel as though we couldn't be more of stereotypical travelers if we tried - but I loved it!

52. Charlie and the Karvan go to... Hanley

Peter Hooper

Saturday 10th September 2016 – and Hanley, Stoke-on-Trent's city centre, was our third and final community workshop of the summer, timed to coincide with the Rio Paralympics. ParalympicsGB had organised a series of city centre carnivals across the UK to celebrate Paralympic sport and Stoke-on-Trent, as the UK's 2016 European City of Sport, had the honour of being selected as one of the carnival locations.

Emma Dawson Varughese and I rendezvoused in the city centre early that morning to go through our by now well-rehearsed set up routine. We left the car and Karvan (Emma's fabulous caravan) on Stafford Street for a couple of minutes while we sussed out our pitch at the top of Tontine Street. After a bit of umming and ahhing about how to get the Karvan in, and a chat with the organiser, we went back to the Karvan to find five buses in a queue behind it and a small delegation of bus drivers marching up the road to find the guilty driver. Luckily I had my Team GB top on and perhaps they mistook me for an Olympian (in my dreams), but they were remarkably forgiving!

Eventually we got the Karvan and marquee set up, and Charlie our 'artist in residence' appeared to help with the banners and pop up stands, before settling down to organise his sketch pads, sharpen pencils and get ready for the day. He didn't know it, but he'd be sketching portraits solid for the next six hours!

We had a cracking position for this workshop, sandwiched between table tennis, goalball, the dance/boccia area, archery and rowing and with plenty of scope for passing city centre trade – and so it proved.

The aim of the event was to get local people, whether disabled or not, to try out a range of new sports with a Paralympic focus. I certainly took advantage, trying out boccia and goalball and proving hapless at both. But back at base, we were swamped with contributors from all backgrounds with so many inspiring stories. And for many of the disabled children present, inspirational parents too.

We knew there were a few local disabled sport club members with great stories too, so part of my job was lining people up to pop over and tell us their stories when we had quieter spells (not that that happened often during the day!). And I was very keen to get Jenny Booth, guest of honour at the event, to pop over for a photo call and to be sketched by Charlie at some stage – Jenny was already a *Sporting Stories* contributor with a great story of her journey to Paralympic gold and bronze medals in swimming and a world record to boot.

Jenny Booth (and supporting cast) at the ParalympicsGB carnival

Jenny Booth sketched by Charlie Walker

Eventually we got all the stories we were after – and what a great selection they were:

The Stories:

<u>Matt Byatt, Masque Theatre company</u>

Once a week I go to Burslem College and attend Break Thro which brings together disabled and non-disabled dancers. The type of dance is contemporary and choreographed and I've been with Break Thro for over 10 years. Over the years I feel Break Thro has helped me improve my dance and choreograph skills. The dance keeps me fit but I'd like to do more!

Matt and his dad, proud owners of an original Charlie Walker drawing

Donna Stanway

On Wednesdays I dance. We start with a warm up then we move to Line Dancing or doing the Grapevine which is my favourite. I also like fast dancing like the Little Mix songs which is really fast! The dancing makes me feel more confident. When I was younger I was really quite shy and now I can take the leading lady roles on stage. I even played Charlene Begood in our play Four Wakes and a Wedding. It was exciting to play this role because of the clothes and the wig I wore. We even sang All Things Bright and Beautiful.

Donna and fellow performers at the Festival

Lillian Beardmore

My love for swimming started in Leek in my school days in the late 1960's and it's never left me. At my best I was swimming 100 lengths in under an hour. I remember early mornings before school and even after school swimming with our coach Mr Lownes, my twin brother used to swim as well. When my kids went to school I did a charity swim to raise money for a local nursery. All the parents didn't know I could swim so I got a sponsorship and they were amazed when I did it! 100 lengths in under an hour.

One of my memories of swimming at school was the visit of Anita Lonsborough at the Mickelson Institute in Leek. Meeting her as a gold medal winner was something amazing. I'm still looking for people who remember that day and might even have photos of the occasion. I would love to hear from anyone. For me swimming keeps you fit, can save your life and for me it created a whole chapter of memories in my life. I can't do much but I can swim!

Helen Stennings, Jack's mum

Rugby Tots - Cheadle Leisure centre

My son Jack goes to Rugby Tots. I was really impressed how Jack followed the teacher's instructions; the teacher was really animated and that helped Jack to follow. It lasted half an hour and he'll be going once a week now.

Jack enjoyed playing with a soft, green rugby ball and he managed to complete the obstacle course many times. Some of the activities really helped develop his sense of balance and co-ordination.

Nathan Hill

For two years I thought I was going to paraglide but the weather just wasn't right however, this year I could do it. It was a very sunny day with a gentle breeze. We climbed Lattrig Hill in a land rover and I saw everything below me - lakes, houses, trees and the woods. In order to get into the flychair for paragliding I had to wear my helmet and it took a while to be fastened in safely - I counted seven straps but there were more!

We had a long wait, waiting for the wind to be correct and then with the help of Dad and another man, the flychair took off. I felt scared, excited but when I was up there I felt more relaxed. I waved back to my Dad and shouted "I love you". Up in the air, I could feel the cold on my face, the wind as well and I felt awesome! My paragliding experience in Keswick this year (2016) is the best experience in my life so far! I would do it again any day! I would!

Nathan and his parents

<u>Ben Adamson</u> (Lilian Beardmore's grandson)

I went to Northwood Stadium for our sports day at school. I won two races and my last one was sprint race.

I had a good start when the whistle blew and ran as fast as I could, and won the race and ran the fastest out of the whole school.

<u>Mia Beardmore</u>

I do gymnastics every day and I like to watch YouTube and learn new skill such as handstands and bars. I practice every day I also go to gymnastics club where I learn to walk on the beam and do a forward roll and go around on the bars.

Even when I walk down the street I see a wall and have to do a handstand. Or bars I have to flip around. I like to show people I can do the splits.

Harry Smith

Not long ago for my birthday I got a basketball net. And I already did hockey but I really struggled so I was getting a wheelchair. So I looked on Google and saw wheelchair basketball and I was interested. Suddenly an email popped up. It was from a wheelchair basketball team. So I started and I was enjoying it so I kept going and going so I've become this good.

Not long ago for my birthday I got a basket ball net. And I already did hockey but I really struggled so I was getting a wheelchair. So I looked on google and saw wheelchair basket ball. And I was intrested suddenly a email popped up. It was from a wheelchair basket ball team. So I started and I was enjoying it so I kept. Going and going so I've become this good.

THE END

Harry smith
age 8

Stoke
Spitfires team

Angela Marie Tyler

Beating the men- they didn't like that

I grew up around Chatterley Whitfield Mining Museum near to Tunstall in Stoke-on-Trent. At the age of 22 I joined the Territorial Army in Burslem. I trained for a few weeks with a friend who was an Army Physical Training Instructor. It came naturally to me as I did cross country at school (James Brindley High and Chell Middle School). Whilst on joining the TA, they said that I had a "knack" for it. They had never seen a woman finish before the men. OK I thought. So I trained harder than ever before. I went to Cardiff Arms Park and the Millennium Stadium in Wales. I got medals and trophies galore. We even did The Krypton Factor. Numerous Assault Courses around England, hill walking in Wales. Competitions in Scotland etc. For three years I had fun and all at the weekend. I got the 'best recruit' award which meant I worked with the new recruits etc. Assisting with First Aid, Marching, Personal help, Drill training etc. A combat Medic and they gave me a rank also: L/CPL Tyler. My sister was so proud. (I have an older twin - 10 minutes older). She was my rock and gave me guidance. Positivity was what I had from Beverly. That 10 minutes older, she was like a mum to me. I worked hard, trained hard and made many friends along the way.

I was in a serious traffic accident whilst on holiday when I was 27 years old and I think being physically fit helped me to survive the serious injuries I obtained: broken arm in three places, head injury, neck injury, leg injury. I manage to fall 1500m above sea level in Turkey and I looked like Medusa (twigs instead of snakes.) Who knows, I think I had a guardian angel. Appropriately, my name means "Heavenly Messenger" in Greek. I've been there too.

Now the future, I work at a home with adults with "Challenging Behaviour" and I use my personal Sporting Story to motivate me every step of the way. My twin sister works there too (In the kitchen): we both work part time.

I have a 15-year-old son Ethan and he is in the Army Cadet Force. He wants to do something medical one day and is in his penultimate year in high school, near to where we live. I hope he reaches his life goal, I've met mine and go on to better things every day. My job keeps me focused. "Challenging Behaviour". They just need someone to talk to who understands them. I also have two dogs that keep me fit, walking them at least three times a day.

To finish, I have been 'Steadfast in Adversity' (*In Ardius Fidelis*) the motto of The Royal Army Medical Corps. I hope you enjoy my story - short though it is.

Cathi Ferrer

Bouldering is a kind of wall-climbing sport but it was invented as a training sport for rock climbing. Bouldering will be part of the 2020 Olympics for the first time. In bouldering, you never climb more than 4.5 metres but unlike rock climbing where there is a harness, you are at the mercy of a crash mat. On that day, I had decided to go bouldering to conquer my fear. What unfolded after only 15 minutes of being at the Centre was not what I expected. Showing my friend how to scale a wall, I missed a hold, I don't remember much about it, only that it was green because I fell backwards and awkwardly on the mat. I heard the crack and I knew then I'd done something. Treated for a broken ankle that needed pinning, three months later the physio discharged me, he was impressed with my recovery and I was so pleased that there was only one place that I wanted to go - The Roaches, there was Hen Cloud to climb!

Matt Fry

I have competed at the highest of my disability within Special Olympics North Staffordshire and Special Olympics Great Britain at football, swimming, basketball, table tennis and Athletics. I have represented my country at European and World level in Mencap sport as well. My biggest memory was winning Gold in 100 metres hurdles at the mini Olympics in Hull 2000. I am a big supporter of grass roots sport and disability sport.

<u>Craig Smith</u>

Jelly Babies

I always enjoyed running at school and it was on one Sports Day that I realised that I was born to run. But football took over during my college days and although you never forgot about running it did take a special person to get me back into my running gear. His name was Alan Haw and he was a really outgoing, caring man. He was loved by everyone. Alan encouraged me to do the Potters 'Arf in 2014; I wasn't sure I could do it, I wanted to do it but I really wasn't sure about how I could train. One of his top tips was eating Jelly Babies- Alan said that he ran from Fenton to Uttoxeter just on the fuel of Jelly Babies. He told me time and time again to be confident, to be myself and just run. I used to volunteer at the club that Alan managed, a small token of appreciation for all of his hard work. Alan passed away just after the Potters 'Arf 2016 but I know that Alan is watching me every time I put on my trainers.

Melissa Walker- Wheelies activity coordinator

I joined Wheelies (a wheelchair sports and activities club) in 2009 through an open day invitation at Tytherington High School in Macclesfield. At the time I had no interest in sport but I went along because of my friend. At first I wondered why I was there because I'd never been into sport and in my mind I had said to myself that I wouldn't like it. But very quickly I changed my mind, I love it now and it has made me realise how lucky I am. I am often described as severely disabled however I don't see myself as such because Wheelies has shown me how other disabled people live. In fact, Wheelies has helped me to understand myself better and be better myself - I mean, to really believe in myself.

I am the activities coordinator which keeps my mind very busy and I look forward to seeing the members develop as individuals and for people to witness that. To see them as individuals with a mind, a heart, an opinion and not simply as people in wheelchairs.

Carla

Horse riding according to Carla

Riding for the disabled hasn't always looked like what it does today. When I took to the saddle I was nine years old and it was the mid-1960s. At that time riding was considered a therapeutic activity; we would wear a belt with hooks on it and people stand either side holding on, making sure you didn't fall. We would be asked to reach forward to touch the horse's ears, its tail and move 360 degrees on the saddle. This latter activity was always my favourite as it was like "freedom" to me. I knew even then that I was capable of more and my parents always supported me. They helped me to be independent by treating me just like my sisters and brother. I believe that my parents' attitude to my disability, especially my mum's attitude instilled in me an independence that really helped me in my riding. This was the era of the "spastic society", "special needs schools" and segregated activities for disabled people. I was fighting against all this - I did not accept these labels or differences.

When I think about today, I think we have come a long way but I'm concerned that we might move backwards before we move forwards; we still have a long way to go. I would like to see more acceptance of disability, equality across society which means that transport, public facilities should be accessible. For me, make the most of life, if something passes across your path take it by both hands and go with it 'cause you might not get another chance.

George Chapman

Wheelchair Basketball: my life

Sport wasn't really part of my life until secondary school when I saw pictures of the "Stoke Spitfires"- a wheelchair basketball club based in Biddulph. I found these images inspirational – it made me think that I could play basketball without limitations. That was years ago now and I feel that watching the other players push themselves has really helped me develop as a person. What might appear as small, insignificant actions to others are real achievements for me and the way I live my life; I now pack my bag and hang it on the back of my wheelchair myself, I have a bath on my own and don't need so much help getting dressed.

Being selected for the regional trials has meant that I've stayed away from home and I enjoyed that opportunity. All in all I've learnt more about myself and I'm more ready to go out and try something new.

George who was a
Vale supporter.
Stoke losing 1-0.

Peter Doyle

Goalball

A turning point in my life was when I was introduced to Goalball by my teacher Stuart Adams in 2009. I started to play nationally at a low level, that took me to new places but most importantly I met new people. When I attended my first Integration camp, I stayed away from home, it was exciting and I felt ready for this new chapter in my life. I remember getting top Goal Scorer and I got to shake hands with the head of GB Men's Goalball; it was a really proud moment for me. Following the camp, I was called to play in Finland as part of GB Youth Team, this was something phenomenal for me. I saw the Goalball Championships whilst I was there; seeing the quality and power of the games was inspiring.

Returning to the UK I was called for a classification where my eyes were tested; it revealed that I was not eligible to play at international level. Despite this news the following day I had to play with my team at an elite level event in Birmingham. Knowing what I knew at that point made playing alongside my team mates a lot harder than usual. I left the sport for a few months. Now I'm back playing although I don't train as much. But all is not lost as I've moved into coaching, which has taken me back to my old school where it all started. I've thought about other sports, my mum has suggested rowing as it requires a similar body build but nothing will be the same as Goalball.

Summerbank Primary School

Peter Hooper

During the summer of 2016, Cox Bank Publishing worked closely with a number of Stoke-on-Trent schools to pilot some sports-writing projects with pupils, as part of our *Sporting Futures* initiative. One of our favourite projects was with Summerbank Primary School in Tunstall, working with Year Two teacher Abi Falconer and her class of budding gymnasts. This was before TeamGB's gymnastics success in Rio, so goodness knows how prospective gymnasts there are across the City now. Abi (or should we say Mrs Falconer) got her class to storyboard their first eight weeks of gymnastics and the results were fantastic. Although they are lovely in their own right, we felt that the storyboards would be a great inspiration for a comic book approach and we are indebted to Gareth Cowlin of Staffordshire University and his students on the Cartoons & Comic Arts degree course for some stunning reinterpretation of the original work. Two examples are shown overleaf, by Jannath (redrawn by Hannah Stanway) and Amy (redrawn by Alessandra Lombardi).

Summerbank Primary School Year 2 Gymnasts – photo courtesy Summerbank Primary School

My First Gymnastics

Janneth

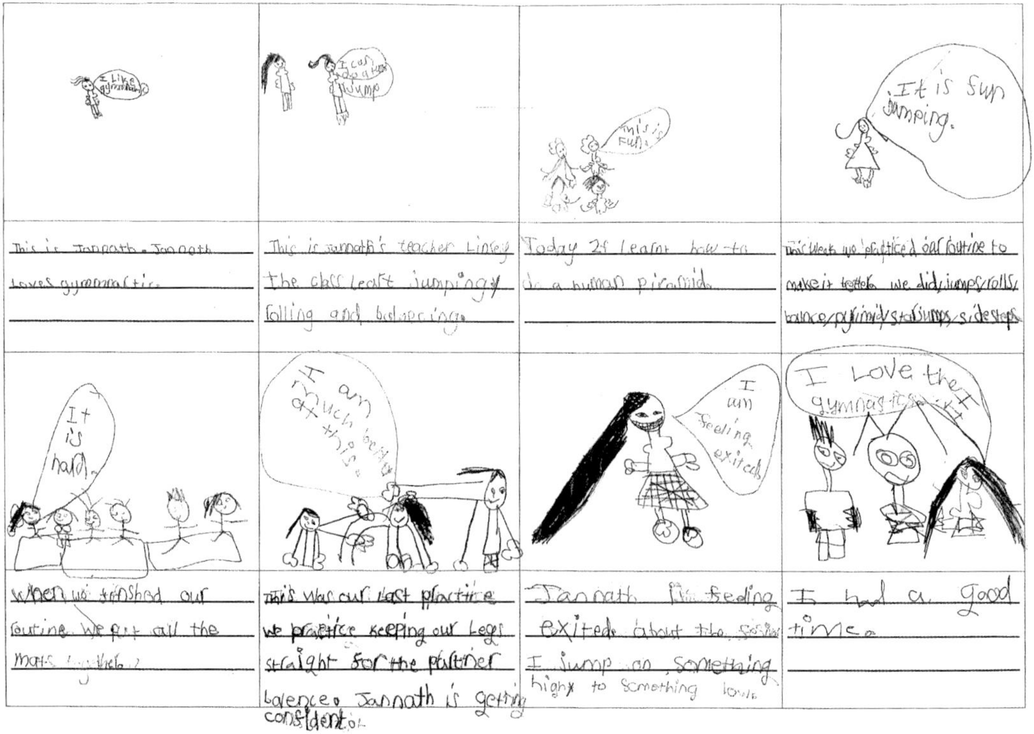

I Like gymnastics

This is Jannath. Jannath loves gymnastics.

I can do a tuck jump

This is Jannath's teacher Linsey. The class learnt jumping, rolling and balancing.

This is Fun.

Today I learnt how to do a human piramid.

It is Sup jumping.

This week we practiced our routine to make it better. We did, jumps, rolls, balance, pyrimid, stairjumps, sidesteps.

It is hard.

When we finished our routine we put all the mats together.

I am much better at this.

This was our last practice we practice keeping our legs straight for the partner balence. Jannath is getting confident.

I am feeling exited.

Jannath feeling exited about the show. I jump on something high to something low.

I Love the gymnastics

I had a good time.

JANNATH
LIKES
GYMNASTICS

JANNATH LEARNED HOW TO
JUMP AND BALANCE

THE CLASS LEARNED
HUMAN PYRAMIDS
AND PRACTICED
FOR THEIR
ROUTINE,
DOING ROLLS
AND
STARJUMPS.
JANNATH AND
HER FRIENDS
ENJOYED PARTNER
BALANCES
AND WORKED AS
A TEAM TO TIDY
AWAY THE MATS.
GYMNASTICS WAS SO
EXCITING AND I LEARNT
LOTS OF NEW THINGS!
HANNAH STANWAY.

My First Gymnastics

Amy

1.	2.	3.	4.
Amy likes gymnastics	I like doing gym		I am better rolls
This is Amy. Amy loves gymnastics.	This is Amy's gym teacher. The class leart rolling, jumeing, balancing.	Today 2F leant how to do a human pyramid.	This week we practiced our routine to make it even better.
5.	**6.**	**7.**	**8. The Festical**
	I'm better at this		I really like gymnastics
When we had finished our routine we put all the mats together and did it as one big group.	This was our last practice. We practiced keeping our legs straight for the partner balance. Amy is getting more confident.	Amy is feeling excited about the festival because I had never performed before.	Amy had a great time at the festival. She was really proud of herself.

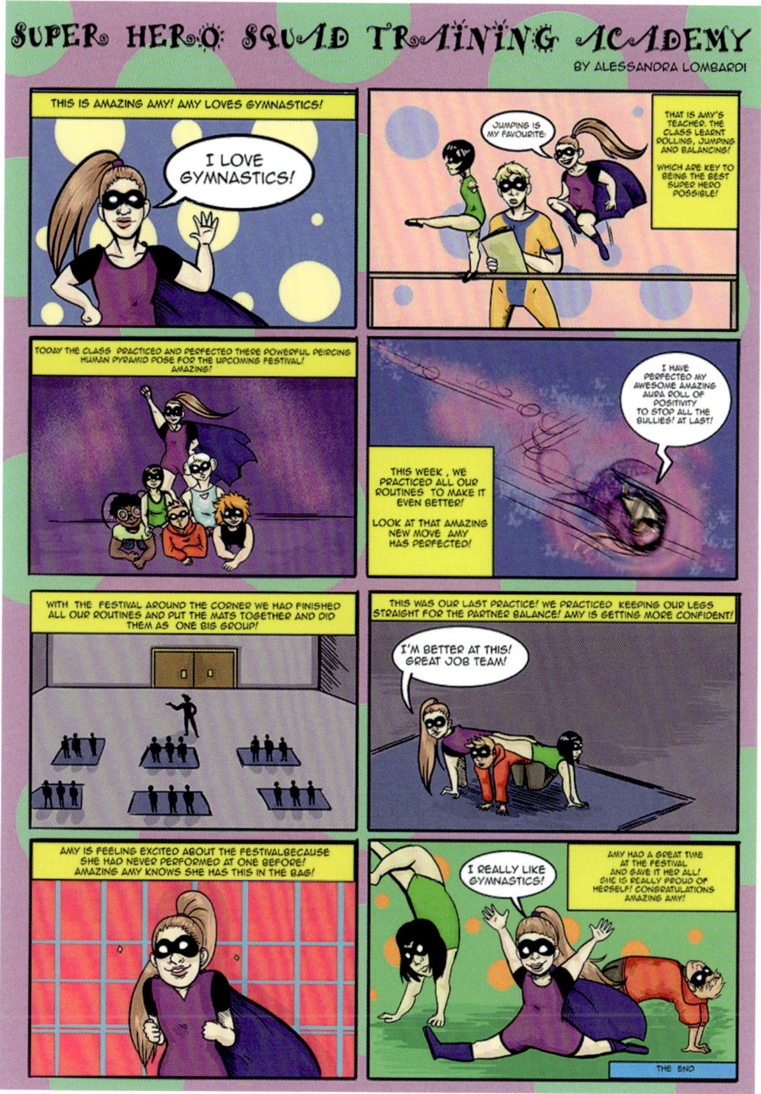
SUPER HERO SQUAD TRAINING ACADEMY
BY ALESSANDRA LOMBARDI
THIS IS AMAZING AMY! AMY LOVES GYMNASTICS!
I LOVE GYMNASTICS!
JUMPING IS MY FAVOURITE!
THAT IS AMY'S TEACHER. THE CLASS LEARNT ROLLING, JUMPING AND BALANCING!
WHICH ARE KEY TO BEING THE BEST SUPER HERO POSSIBLE!
TODAY THE CLASS PRACTICED AND PERFECTED THERE POWERFUL PEIRCING HUMAN PYRAMID POSE FOR THE UPCOMING FESTIVAL! AMAZING!
THIS WEEK , WE PRACTICED ALL OUR ROUTINES TO MAKE IT EVEN BETTER!
LOOK AT THAT AMAZING NEW MOVE AMY HAS PERFECTED!
I HAVE PERFECTED MY AWESOME AMAZING AURA ROLL OF POSITIVITY TO STOP ALL THE BULLIES! AT LAST!
WITH THE FESTIVAL AROUND THE CORNER WE HAD FINISHED ALL OUR ROUTINES AND PUT THE MATS TOGETHER AND DID THEM AS ONE BIG GROUP!
THIS WAS OUR LAST PRACTICE! WE PRACTICED KEEPING OUR LEGS STRAIGHT FOR THE PARTNER BALANCE! AMY IS GETTING MORE CONFIDENT!
I'M BETTER AT THIS! GREAT JOB TEAM!
AMY IS FEELING EXCITED ABOUT THE FESTIVALBECAUSE SHE HAD NEVER PERFORMED AT ONE BEFORE! AMAZING AMY KNOWS SHE HAS THIS IN THE BAG!
I REALLY LIKE GYMNASTICS!
AMY HAD A GREAT TIME AT THE FESTIVAL AND GAVE IT HER ALL! SHE IS REALLY PROUD OF HERSELF! CONGRATULATIONS AMAZING AMY!
THE END

Afterword – a View From ACES Europe

John Swanson

ACES – the European Capitals & Cities of Sport Federation – is the body which awarded the city of Stoke-on-Trent its 2016 European City of Sport status. As part of the award, a team from ACES, led by John Swanson, Vice President of ACES Europe, undertook a review of the city's implementation of its City of Sport year and how it had gone. This is John's perspective of the year.

The ACES inspection team were extremely impressed with the effectiveness of the implementation of their award the European City of Sport 2016. Stoke-on-Trent clearly has sport and healthy activities as part of its core provision, and we saw for ourselves sport being used to help build social cohesion, particularly in more disadvantaged parts of the city. It is good to note that despite challenging financial circumstances Stoke-on-Trent has continued to invest in the benefits of access to and participation in sport. This is highlighted by a true partnership approach, with all that brings in terms of attracting extra investment for the benefit of the city.

We were particularly impressed by the additional funding of nearly £4m that the city bought to bear, to ensure that a long-term legacy was left for the people of the city after the year of sport was finished. Impressively, this included external funding of almost £1m secured from key partners.

In terms of celebrating the award the City successfully hosted many special events including:

- 1966 World Cup Winners' Gala Dinner.
- Aviva Women's Tour.
- UK Triathlon.
- England v Greece table tennis international.
- ParalympicsGB Carnival.
- The Lord Mayor's Games.

Equally, we also very impressed with the number of smaller community events that were delivered in parks and community centres. It is encouraging to see initiatives underway to further volunteer development and good practices in sports clubs.

In conclusion then, the ACES Europe team were delighted to see that the legacy of the award will continue – already many international and community events are planned for 2017 and beyond. Stoke-on-Trent is a true city of sports and their year of sport was one of the best we have witnessed to date. It will certainly be a hard act to follow!

ACES Europe: left to right Lukas Vorel, John Swanson and Kevin O'Connor on their inspection tour of Stoke-on-Trent, 2016 European City of Sport

Photograph and Illustration Credits

Forward, page 12 – illustration reproduced with permission of Simon Chubb, Scartoons
Chapter 1 – photographs by Peter Hooper, except image of Lizzie Tench in Rio (page 22) courtesy Lizzie Tench, and Dragon Boat racing (page 24) courtesy Stoke-on-Trent City Council
Chapter 2 – images courtesy Andy Baggaley
Chapter 3 – images courtesy Zara Bailey
Chapter 5 – images courtesy Andy Barratt
Chapter 6 – images by Peter Hooper. Photo of Meg Higgins (pages 44, 45) with permission of Sue Higgins. Photo of Gemma Woodworth and children (page 48) with permission of Gemma Woodworth.
Chapter 7 – image courtesy Erin Boddice
Chapter 8 – images courtesy Jenny Booth
Chapter 9 – cartoon by Duncan Bourne, reproduced with permission of the artist
Chapter 10 – artwork by Kate Ackley, reproduced with permission of the artist
Chapter 11 – images courtesy of Anthony Bunn. Image on page 72 taken from the cover of DUCK magazine.
Chapter 12 – images courtesy Daniel Cartwright, except one on page 77 courtesy Hillside Primary School
Chapter 13 – images courtesy Lucas and Jason Christer
Chapter 14 – image courtesy Jeremy Cliffe
Chapter 15 – artwork on page 85 by Gaz Williams, reproduced with permission of the artist; image on page 87 with permission of Viv Cotton
Chapter 16 – image by Peter Hooper
Chapter 17 – image courtesy of Hillside Primary School
Chapter 18 – images courtesy Jean Gough
Chapter 19 – image courtesy SA Images
Chapter 20 – images courtesy Andrew Heaward
Chapter 22 – images courtesy New Pixels Photography (except page 117, Peter Hooper)
Chapter 23 – artwork by Paine Proffitt, reproduced with permission of the artist. Image on page 120 courtesy Jan Garner
Chapter 24 – images courtesy Emma Jackson
Chapter 25 – images courtesy Glenn James
Chapter 26 – image reproduced with permission from Wrestling Heritage
Chapter 27 – artwork by Dave Flitcroft, reproduced with permission of the artist

Chapter 28 – image by Peter Hooper, with permission of Becky Latham
Chapter 29 – image by Peter Hooper
Chapter 30 – image on page 145 courtesy of Bryan Dale; images on pages 150 and 151 courtesy Mick Hall
Chapter 31 – image on page 156 Peter Hooper; artwork on page 157 courtesy Charlie Walker.
Chapter 32 – image courtesy Jane Longmore
Chapter 33 – image courtesy the Loska family
Chapter 35 – image courtesy Nigel Moore
Chapter 36 – image courtesy Stoke-on-Trent City Council
Chapter 38 – images courtesy Janet Mason
Chapter 40 – image courtesy Mick Hall
Chapter 41 – images courtesy Zoe Robinson
Chapter 42 – image courtesy Ken Rushton
Chapter 43 – artwork by Steve Shaw, reproduced with permission of the artist; image on page 191 courtesy Steve Shaw
Chapter 44 – images courtesy Laura Malkin Photography
Chapter 45 – images courtesy Pat Sinclair
Chapter 46 – images courtesy Angela Smith: image page 199 also courtesy www.squashmad.com
Chapter 47 – image courtesy Jeremy Snape, www.sportingedge.com
Chapter 49 – images courtesy Liz Tideswell
Chapter 50 – image courtesy St Joseph's College
Chapter 51 – image on page 213 with courtesy of B.P.M. Harris; all other images courtesy Matthew Wilcock
Chapter 52 – images courtesy Charlie Walker; all drawings courtesy of Charlie Walker and the subjects
Chapter 53 – images courtesy Summerbank Primary School; artwork on page 245 courtesy Hannah Stanway, page 247 courtesy Alessandra Lombardi
Chapter 54 – image courtesy Stoke-on-Trent City Council

Page 252 – image courtesy Stoke-on-Trent City Council

Back cover – images courtesy of the contributors: clockwise from top left Peter Hooper, Jan Garner, Mo Hastings, Liz Tideswell, Peter Hooper (boxer, climber and Lizzie Armistead), Laura Malkin Photography, Stoke-on-Trent City Council, Peter Hooper, Andrew Heaward, Harry Pointon (Special Olympics).

Front cover artwork by Gaz Williams

Cover design by John Mainwaring, MarketingBiDesign